QUEERING THE WAY

TREVOR
SCHMIDT

THE
LOUD &
QueeR
ANTHOLOGY

Edited by Darrin Hagen

BRINDLE
& GLASS

Brindle & Glass Publishing Ltd.
brindleandglass.com

LIBRARY AND ARCHIVES CANADA CATALOGUING IN PUBLICATION
Queering the way : the Loud and Queer
anthology / [edited by] Darrin Hagen.

Issued also in electronic formats.
ISBN 978-1-897142-58-5

1. Music-halls (Variety-theaters, cabarets, etc.)—Alberta—
Edmonton. 2. Performance art—Alberta—Edmonton.
3. Gays and the performing arts—Alberta—Edmonton.
I. Hagen, Darrin, 1964–

PN1969.C3Q44 2011   792.709712334   C2011-904182-0

Editor: Heather Sangster, Strong Finish
Cover photo: Ian Jackson/Epic. Make up: Neon and James Ross
Design: Pete Kohut
Author photo: Charles McDuff Gillis

Brindle & Glass is pleased to acknowledge the financial support for its publishing
program from the Government of Canada through the Canada Book Fund, Canada
Council for the Arts, and the Province of British Columbia through the British
Columbia Arts Council and the Book Publishing Tax Credit.

For Ruth Smillie, for her vision of the future . . .

And for Kevin Hendricks, for his commitment to honouring what has come before.

CONTENTS

Darrin Hagen 1 Introduction

Queering the Way Into Forbidden Landscapes

Rosemary Rowe 17 Anne and Diana Were
TOTALLY DOING IT

Darrin M. McCloskey 31 The Confession

Ruth DyckFehderau 37 Whiter Than Snow

Nathan Cuckow 43 STANDupHOMO (an excerpt)

Susan Jeremy 51 Touring and Scoring:
Tales of a Lesbian Stand-Up Comic

Nick Green 57 Chicken Mom

Laurie MacFayden 67 for theodore

Norm Sacuta 71 Traffic

Queering the Way by Voicing Otherness

steen (christina) starr 77 Holding . . . a poetic monologue
(an excerpt)

Marc Colbourne 81 The Interview

Susan Holbrook 89 Why Do I Feel Guilty in the
Changeroom at Britannia Pool?

R.W. Gray 95 Sweet Tooth

Berend McKenzie 103 tassels

Queering the Way by Creating New Artistic Landscapes

Peter Field 113 The Unrestrained Homosexual

Kristy Harcourt 117 The Flood

Trevor Schmidt 123 Birthday

Michaela Washburn 133 The River

Beau Coleman 137 continental divide: a video installation
in 16 sequences (an excerpt)

Chandra Mayor 149 Maybe

Gerald Osborn 153 Skinflute Sonata

T.L. Cowan 169 This is a picture of me

Trevor Anderson 177 The Island

Acknowledgments 183

About the editor 184

Introduction
DARRIN HAGEN

In 1991, Alberta was talking about very Queer things.

In what would become a pivotal moment in the uphill battle for equal rights for Alberta's population of sexual minorities, Delwin Vriend had just been fired from his teaching position at the religious King's College in Edmonton. Being gay, the college administration rationalized, went against church teachings. Vriend had no way to challenge his dismissal under Alberta's antiquated Individual Rights Protection Act, as sexual orientation was not on the list of protected subsections of society. So began the long road to the Supreme Court.

At the same time, a controversial lesbian piercing art exhibit by the Kiss and Tell Collective had riled up some provincial governmental powers. In reaction to that exhibit, the powers-that-be in Calgary were arguing that decisions about arts funding should rest on the shoulders of the people. Ideally, they suggested, each community should set its own moral threshold and be asked to examine its own standards in arts funding.

Suddenly, Alberta was having a conversation about "community standards."

Community standards became a catch phrase for a government refusing to make decisions that could cause controversy; some felt it would become another way to say censorship. It *was* a way for the socially conservative to avoid specific statements about why a certain piece of art was not funded and to off-load the decision-making process onto the community hosting the cultural event/work of art/show.

The Alberta government's uneasy relationship with anything *not* straight-white-male-cowboy was already well documented. But the willingness with which they off-loaded responsibility was surprising. The debate raged—arts organizations feared the worst, imagining small-town councils quashing anything out of the ordinary.

It was in this chilly artistic/political climate that the artistic director of Catalyst Theatre, Ruth Smillie, decided to launch Alberta's first Queer arts event.

A gathering of Queer culture was radically new, and unusual in that the drive to create such an event originated outside of that community. The Gay, Lesbian, Bisexual, Transgender, Queer, and Questioning (GLBTQQ) community (there were less letters in that acronym back in the early 1990s) had organized Pride events, humble but growing—early Gay Pride Parades in Edmonton were small affairs that travelled down out-of-the-way side streets. There had been Queer art, and some of it had been successful—playwright Brad Fraser's career had taken off, as had the international success of his 1989 play *Unidentified Human Remains and the True Nature of Love*. The Names Project (Canada's AIDS Quilt) had been displayed twice in a very high-profile manner as part of the Works Visual Arts Festival, with hundreds of quilt memorial panels taking over the giant lobby of the Citadel Theatre. And there was definitely a new wave of Queer artists emerging at Edmonton's Fringe Festival (our own Guys in Disguise included, which in 1987 became the first Edmonton drag troupe to go public in a big way). But there were no real "community" events focusing specifically on the arts and artists.

Back then, Catalyst Theatre had a mandate to create theatre

designed to reach marginalized communities. Smillie had the theatre, the staff, and some contacts within the academic Queer writing community. I, with my partner/publicist Kevin Hendricks, had the connection to Edmonton's Queer audience through decades of output in the community, first from programming entertainment at the legendary Flashback nightclub and then by producing theatre and launching events that mixed art and activism such as Edmonton's first Day Without Art, part of a national movement to mark World AIDS Day, during which theatres and galleries were shrouded across the city.

Smillie approached us about her idea, looking for a connection to the community. And from that conversation emerged the Loud & Queer (L&Q) Cabaret. It was a one-night show, rehearsed for two days, featured about eight writers, and sold out completely with no press, no previews, no media at all—in fact, media weren't allowed in the building while the event was on. Word circulated the way the Queer community always kept itself in the loop—from individual to individual, from barstool to barstool.

Two decades later, L&Q still thrives. Now it's two full (very full) evenings of artists, boasting newcomers and veterans alike, and spanning every artistic discipline. Finding an audience was never an issue, but the event was not without its struggles.

The impact of the media's portrayal of Queer art hit home in 1995, year four of L&Q's existence, when the event received its first televised media coverage. Local station ITV Edmonton sent a reporter and videographer to interview writer James Tyler Irvine, who was contributing to L&Q for his third year in a row. Not only was he filmed in rehearsal as the actors worked on his script, but he was filmed working in his home. Smillie and the Catalyst administration team assumed that the story would be a standard artistic preview, publicizing the burgeoning event.

However, when the story aired, it was part of a "news" series entitled "You Paid For It." The piece claimed that tax dollars were being used to create "controversial" art. Jason Kenney, then-mouthpiece for the Canadian Taxpayers Federation, opined, "Nobody has a right to a government grant. We do have a right not to be discriminated against on certain bases enumerated in the Charter but that doesn't include a right to throw 30,000 tax dollars away on a ridiculous excuse for theatre."

Smillie stood firm, countering with "I'm not sure that Loud & Queer is particularly controversial unless you're homophobic." She also challenged the notion that *any* tax dollars were being used to sustain the event, offering up proof that L&Q was supported entirely by ticket sales and community sponsors.

Not only was the story misinformed, it also appeared to have crossed some other ethical lines. It "outed" everyone on camera in the story. This might not have been a problem had everyone in the story been Queer. In fact, none of the actors performing that year were gay or lesbian, despite the prominent "Gay Actor" subtitle that ITV placed under the images of the actors reading the scripts.

The backlash was small but instant. Several sponsors of L&Q immediately contacted ITV and threatened to boycott any business that advertised on its channel. According to the final Canadian Broadcast Standards Council report on the incident, the reporter faced disciplinary action, and the news team re-evaluated the way they would represent items—including acknowledging that the banner title "You Paid For It" could well have been inflammatory. However, they disagreed that the reporter was compelled to reveal the angle she was pursuing, stating, "The Council does not consider that a distortion occurred in this instance."

It was a short fight, but it was a fight.

ITV took the backlash seriously and examined how it handled the story. The final decision promised that "a result of this unfortunate incident will be a redoubling of efforts to scrutinize news stories before they go to air." The power of the words was crystal clear—and L&Q had forced media to examine how they used those words.

It was Smillie's final year at Catalyst Theatre. She left Edmonton, becoming the artistic director of the Globe Theatre in Regina, Saskatchewan. A few years later she called me and asked, "Do you want to come and host a Regina version of L&Q?" I jumped at the chance, and I was lucky to witness the steps that Regina's community made in those years. Smillie maintains that L&Q was instrumental in elevating both the profile and the understanding of the Queer community in Regina, a claim that applies to the community in Edmonton as well.

After a difficult transition as Catalyst Theatre changed mandates to explore other artistic modes, the new artistic directors dropped L&Q from the theatre's programming. Without a theatre company proper to host the event, L&Q quietly disappeared for a season. This was "the dark year."

In 1996, Jacquie Richardson, who had worked at Catalyst during Smillie's tenure, approached Guys in Disguise about reviving the event. She was now the general manager for Workshop West Theatre (WWT), under the new artistic director, David Mann. WWT's mandate was the creation and development of new Canadian theatre. Soon enough, the next generation of L&Q was under way, generating waves artistically. Writers displayed a new sense of purpose, and work presented at L&Q began to spread to other venues and cultural institutions. And since the re-launch, L&Q has been produced every November without fail.

A path had been Queered. And so the community moved forward.

The existence of Loud & Queer became the launching pad for many now-prominent Queer writers/artists in Edmonton. As those Edmonton artists relocate, the influence of L&Q spreads and multiplies. Artists who took their first steps at the event are now published or produced—in some cases, internationally.

The millions of words that have spilled off the stage and into the minds of eager and loyal audience members have, in fact, changed history. L&Q not only teaches artists (myself included) that their stories matter, but it also teaches the world around us that we have something to say. It's a powerful testament to the enduring power of the voice.

So the L&Q audience heard homo-rap music that ended up gracing the stages of Off-Broadway New York. They listened to stories about Edmonton drag queens that are now discussed and taught across North America and Europe. They witnessed pronouncements by individuals who would affect the fight for equality in Alberta. The audience saw huge shifts in artistic careers as writers and drag queens and filmmakers took daring leaps into the unknown. These artists landed expertly and upright and confident, assured of success not only by what they had learned about the power of their vision, but by the support of the producing companies, the dozens of faithful sponsors, the audience, the directors, and the actors who consistently brought their most inspired work to the stage.

A new community standard had emerged. At Regina's L&Q, writer Brita Lind watched her work being performed as her partner went into the hospital to give birth to their first child. I grabbed a cellphone and we called the mom-to-be in the hospital, the entire Globe Theatre audience cheering on the creation of a new family.

The L&Q audience was also able to listen as author and columnist Dan Savage gave sex advice from the stage. They heard openly gay (and renowned) puppeteer Ronnie Burkett talk about touring his marionettes around the world. And—in a particularly riveting cross-gender turnabout—improv genius Mark Meer's alter-ego, Susanna Patchouli, interviewed trans porn star Buck Angel. For the uninitiated, that's a straight man dressed as a woman interviewing a woman who has become a man—and kept all the original plumbing. "I like my pussy," claimed Buck Angel. "Yes, I am a cat fancier myself!" replied Susanna.

In the hothouse environment of L&Q, a frankness emerged, sometimes a defiance. The word spread. The work spread. The way branched repeatedly, creating new paths to success.

All of this happened during a tenure of the provincial Conservative dynasty that attempted, at every step of the battle, to hinder the advancement of equality for Alberta's population of sexual minorities: battling lesbian foster moms in court, refusing to budge on same-sex marriage or individual rights protection until the Supreme Court of Canada declared their stance unconstitutional.

Since that time, many changes have occurred: legal protection, activism with results, an opening of media, of message, of minds. Supreme Court judges agreed with our instinctive expectation of fair treatment. The tide changed, finally. And we all felt that change as it swept through our lives. It was like coming up for air after decades of holding our breath.

Every time a community gathers and shares its stories, every time the words are spoken out loud, history changes inexorably to make space, to allow for the new thought to exist. The ripples that move out from there are small but unstoppable—the proof evident in the 2009 launch of Edmonton's now-annual Exposure Queer Arts and Cultural Festival. Every success stands on the shoulders of those who came before.

Loud & Queer has launched writers, performers, musicians, comedians, and filmmakers. It has featured dancers, singer-songwriters, monologists, spoken-word artists, poets, and belly dancers. Opera. Heavy metal. Drag queens. Drag kings. Performance artists. Activists. Politicians.

And now, this anthology: a permanent record of a pivotal time in Alberta's Queer history, captured by the imaginations of a courageous and outspoken population of artists.

This collection of writing is an attempt to present a snapshot of the event. It is just a taste of the never-ending smorgasbord of art that has been paraded across the stage. It won't tell the whole story because that would take twenty years. It won't give you the experience of the sudden surprise when a new artist commands the stage like an expert. It won't show you openly gay Edmonton city councillor Michael Phair gleefully heckling me as I attempt to host the show. It won't let you feel what it's like to walk through protesters in Regina to see a show about your life and read misspelled signs proclaiming: "Sodamy kills more Canadians a year than handguns!"

It won't allow you to watch my legendary Drag Mother, Lulu LaRude, and I, both in full glamour drag, calling up homophobic politicians and leaving messages of pride and defiance on their answering machines with a crowd cheering us in the background.

But it will allow you to hear the voices. The stories.

In selecting the twenty-two artists that populate this anthology, I was forced to make difficult choices. I had to leave out some fine and pivotal work by very talented people. Some of the early work is lost to history, or trapped in dead computers. Early contributors such as Janice Williamson, Daniel Cunningham, Genevieve Varze, James Tyler Irvine, Delvina Grieg, Stephen Dyson, Jocelyn Brown, Brita Lind, Michael Vonn, and dozens of others responded to the themes and battles of the time, bringing inspired work to an eager community. All successes that followed are due to these artists stepping forward to take a chance on a fledgling idea. Their imaginations led the way, and due respect has to be given to these pioneers.

In the work collected here, you will see how a new generation of Queer writers are not only writing about Queer and are creating new spaces for themselves, using their sense of otherness to define their unique experiences, but are also writing themselves into spaces they were previously excluded from.

These three distinct themes emerged as I selected the work, and I have arranged the writing accordingly. The results are honest, unflinching, and often surprising.

Queering the Way Into Forbidden Landscapes

A leading Canadian literary icon is recast and reimagined in comedic writer Rosemary Rowe's clever and hilarious "Anna & Diana Were TOTALLY Doing It," where a closer reading of the term *bosom friends* suggests that Anne—she of Green Gables fame—seems positively in lust with Diana and wastes no opportunity to transform ordinary moments in girlhood into afternoons of intimate exploration.

In Darrin M. McCloskey's "The Confession," the privacy of the confession booth becomes a place where desire—and confusion about the etiquette of the confessional—is explored. The narrator's indecision in matters regarding sexual categories has him communicating with his priest as if the confessional were a therapist's couch instead of a holy place. It's obvious he has little to confess, yet he feels compelled to confess that he doesn't really know how to confess.

Ruth DyckFehderau's "Whiter Than Snow" takes on a different rite of religious passage—the baptism—and in her hands it transforms into a setting for exploring sexual maturity. DyckFehderau's intimate details that belie the upstanding sanctimony of small-town religious ritual are sharply drawn and telling—a young adult is beginning to see the world around her for what it is, not for what it is being presented as.

In "STANDupHOMO," playwright Nathan Cuckow uses the fractured and psychotic character of a stand-up comic as a way to deny—and embrace—some hard-learned stereotypes. The shattered fragments of truth and lies leave the listener gasping with laughter, even as we ask ourselves, Is the comedian lying to us or is he lying to himself?

For real-life comedian Susan Jeremy, stand-up comedy is a dangerous—and sometimes sexy—place in which to make a living. In "Touring and Scoring: Tales of a Lesbian Stand-Up Comic," she pulls back the curtains on the closeted world of the comedy club in decades past. Long before Ellen and Will and Grace became household names, comedy was a type of work that required a modicum of discretion for queers. But sometimes all caution gets thrown to the wind in order to seize sexual opportunity.

Playwright Nick Green assesses the family unit in "Chicken Mom"—a heartwarming and insightful portrayal of a mother in the throes of coping with her son's new gay identity, trying to resist her mother-hen instincts in order to allow the boy to experience his coming-out in his own way, as opposed to the self-help books she has devoured like so much chicken soup.

Poet Laurie MacFayden's "for theodore" tells an all-too familiar tale for anyone who attended a funeral and witnessed the white-washing of a life story—and the erasure of "queer" from the eulogy. MacFayden bravely puts the real story back in place.

Norm Sacuta's comic poem "Traffic" shows the inevitable clash of two very different Alberta cultures as a hockey rally down Edmonton's main street comes face to face with the reigning Queen of Edmonton as she struts her stuff to the delight of Her People cheering from the gay bar above. Hockey Kings and a Drag Queen negotiate sharing the street.

Queering the Way by Voicing Otherness

Writer/poet steen (christina) starr explores the dynamics of

lesbian longing and loss in the sensual excerpt from "Holding . . .
a poetic monologue"—originally performed as beat poetry with
a live conga player.

Marc Colbourne's "The Interview" is part of a collection-
in-progress that details the gay immigrant experience—a story
within a story that paints an idyllic portrait of love in a small
Central American village and a terrifying vision of danger and
exclusion.

In Susan Holbrook's "Why Do I Feel Guilty in the Changeroom
at Britannia Pool?" she takes a moment of extreme normalcy and
paints it as an adventures, full of secret longings and thrills.

R.W. Gray's "Sweet Tooth" shows the casual dinner party for
what it really is—a tangled and complex mixture of emotions
and rituals, where the flavours change as the ingredients are
combined.

In emerging playwright Berend McKenzie's "tassels," two
forms of "otherness" collide in one story—a young boy's obsession with a pink sparkly skipping rope changes to shame when it
becomes an object of torture in the hands of bullies.

Queering the Way by Creating New Artistic Landscapes

Visual artist Peter Field's minimalist "The Unrestrained
Homosexual" reveals that Queer can be as uneventful as any
hetero life—indeed, nothing ever happens. Field has the distinc-
tion of creating one of the first bona fide "hits" of L&Q, and it has
been presented several times over the years.

In writer/activist Kristy Harcourt's "The Flood," a work of art
inspired by fag-bashing becomes a victim of its own machinery.
She explores, in a few paragraphs, her steps into her new community, then into a piece of political art.

In writer/director Trevor Schmidt's "Birthday," Queer is sec-
ondary. The focus of the storyteller is on the missing brother, the

mystery of how he disappeared, and the marking of an anniversary of loss.

Likewise, writer/performer Michaela Washburn's "The River" is heartfelt, composed in moments of grief, tapping into an ancient symbolism, a flow of emotion that cannot be stopped—nor should it be.

In experimental artist Beau Coleman's excerpt from "continental divide," the words shift and swirl, colliding and collapsing under and over each other. Originally presented as a video installation, four TV screens show only a mouth speaking sparse, stark, and overlapping phrases.

Short-story artist Chandra Mayor's "Maybe" puts a solitary and shattered woman in a desperate moment—the aftermath of being included in a group whose purpose is vigil and hope. The hope disappears in the lonely moments after the vigil, and she reaches out—just in time.

Gerald Osborn's "Skinflute Sonata" places the eternally glum and shy middle-aged hero in the most typical of gay bars, where he realizes that even within his own community, he is an outsider. It is "man's best friend," in the form of his optimistic and randy penis, that pep-talks him into not giving up and into embracing his inner misfit.

Spoken-word artist T.L. Cowan's "This is a picture of me" is a series of simple, narrated snapshots. She moves the reader forward through momentous shifts in her thinking, socio-political alignment, and inevitable sense of loss as memories are triggered. When performed, the slideshow is blank: the click of the projector and the bright empty white frame move us forward, eager to "witness" the next picture—even though the pictures are only words.

Lastly, filmmaker Trevor Anderson's "The Island" is a short animated film that wrestles with the oft-cited redneck phrase "put them all on an island" and follows the logic to imagine a sensual fag party island with free drinks and medication and glorious prideful volcanic sacrifices—and then returns to cold reality, the empty prairie that he calls home.

That home is a different place now, transformed by the stories that have Queered the way, transforming my province for the better, forever.

Queering the Way

Into Forbidden Landscapes

Romantic Friends
NADIYA VLASHCHENKO, DREAMSTIME.COM

Anne and Diana Were TOTALLY DOING IT
ROSEMARY ROWE

Rose, an academic, stands at a lectern, preparing to make her presentation. Behind her is a screen on which her PowerPoint slides are projected. The title slide reads "Romantic Friendship in the 19th Century." Beside her is a playing area with a low bench and sundry props: some fake flowers, a small bowl, an old-fashioned quilt.

Rose: Romantic friendship in the nineteenth century. Was it good clean fun? Or was it merely a duck blind for the love that dare not moan its name softly in the night to one's school chum?

Most historians agree that passionate, exclusive, and intimate friendships between women, in centuries outside our own, were looked upon as normal and compatible with heterosexual marriage by anglo-European society. As feminist historian Maeve Davidson said, "No dick involved, no harm done." I paraphrase Davidson.

While it is reasonable to assume that not all of those romantic friendships were as innocent in nature as society believed them to be, some historians, Louise Diggleby among them, assert that instances of sexual relationships between romantic friends were not only occasional but irrelevant. I disagree.

I contend that far more romantic friendships than we previously imagined evolved into something too private to bring up at the quilting bee. The majority of my evidence for this contention is found in specific works of fiction produced by female authors of the nineteenth and early twentieth century.

I believe that these literary works, when read through the correct lens, offer us clues as to what was really going on under the goose down.

Louisa May Alcott's *Work: A Story of Experience* and *An Old-Fashioned Girl* are part of this canon, as well as "Martha's Lady" by Sarah Orne Jewett and Catherine Virginia Russell's subtle masterpiece, *Vanessa of Beaver Mountain*.

No books of the period, however, are as subversive and rich in codified lesbian information as Lucy Maud Montgomery's classic novels of nineteenth-century girl-hood, *Anne of Green Gables* and its sequels.

I intend to prove, through a hermeneutical analysis, that author Lucy Maud Montgomery left hidden messages in her texts that clearly indicate to the cognizant reader that her beloved characters, the romantic, or "bosom" friends, Anne Shirley and Diana Barry were, in fact, totally doing it.

As no literary exploration would be complete without speculative re-enactments, I have engaged the services of two actors from our theatre department to demonstrate what I believe are some key scenes from the novels. These scenes have been written with an eye to expose the subtext of these encounters.

Two women, Renee and Rebecca, enter and take their places on stage. They're dressed as Anne Shirley and Diana Barry in approximations of nineteenth-century garb.

Renee *(gestures toward Renee)* will be playing the part of Diana and Rebecca *(gestures toward Rebecca)* will be playing the part of Anne.

We begin with a scene that I believe marks a significant moment of discovery for the girls. Anne has accidentally got Diana drunk on currant wine, thinking the wine was raspberry cordial. As a result, Diana's mother, Mrs. Barry, has forbidden Anne and Diana to see each other ever again.

Did Mrs. Barry suspect, as the reader does, that Anne and Diana were drinking *their* currant wine . . . from the furry cup? Observe.

SCENE ONE:

Diana: I'll never have another bosom friend—I don't want to have. I couldn't love anybody as I love you.

Anne: Oh, Diana—do you LOVE me?

Diana: Why, of course I do. Didn't you know that?

Anne: No. I thought you LIKED me of course, but I never hoped you'd LOVE me. Oh, this is wonderful! It's a ray of light that will forever shine on the darkness of a path severed from thee, Diana. Oh, just say it once again.

Diana: I love you devotedly, Anne, and I always will.

Anne: And I will always love thee, Diana.

They clasp hands.

Diana: When we hold hands, I feel queer inside . . . like I've eaten a dish of Mrs. Lynde's warm peach preserves, all sweet and . . . wet . . . and slippery.

Anne: Why, Diana . . . you're so flushed. And your breast is . . . heaving.

Diana: Yours too. I hope it isn't the scarlet fever.

Anne: Oh, Diana!

They embrace passionately.

Anne: If it is the scarlet fever, we'd best take all our clothes off and bathe in the cool water of this stream.

Diana: But what if I slip on the rocks? You know I'm not a strong swimmer, Anne.

Anne: I'll keep my arms close around you, beloved. Then if you slip, we'll drown together. An eternal embrace. Oh, just to think of it gives me a thrill. A queer, down below sort of thrill. Do you ever get a thrill like that, Diana?

Diana: Not before I met you, Anne. Oh, I feel faint. We'd better hurry. Mother will miss me if I'm gone too long.

Anne: Let's get you out of that tight corset.

End scene.

Rose: Thank you.

This Meier/Mayes chart outlines the five stages of the romantic friendship, as demonstrated by the characters of Anne Shirley and Diana Barry.

Five Stages of Romantic Friendship

Longing for Close Female Friend

Linking Arms

Avowals of Love

Sleepovers

Handjobs

a. Longing for a close female friend (evinced by Anne)

Anne tells Marilla that she longs for a "bosom" friend.

b. Linking arms when walking

c. Passionate avowals of never-ending love

Which we have just witnessed.

d. Sleepovers

Once Anne has performed a service to the Barry family by saving their younger daughter, Minnie May, from dying of the croup, she is invited to a ball and to stay over with Diana as a reward. Again, the reader exchanges a knowing glance with Montgomery, as we know what is coming next:

e. Handjobs

Once Stage E has been reached and surpassed, however, Montgomery shows the reader that things have become more complicated for Anne and Diana. This next scene occurs a few years later in their relationship, when Anne returns home from teachers' college. Though they had sworn to love each other until death, jealousy, ever the hallmark of a lesbian relationship, rears its ugly head.

SCENE TWO:

Anne: Oh, Diana, it's good to be back again. Isn't that breath of mint delicious? And that tea rose—why, it's a song and a hope and a prayer all in one. And it's good to see you again, Diana!

Diana: I thought you liked that Stella Maynard better than me. Josie Pye told me you did. Josie said you were infatuated with her.

Anne laughs and pelts Diana with faded June lilies.

Anne: Stella Maynard is the dearest girl in the world but one, and you are that one, Diana. I love you more than ever and I've so many things to tell you.

Diana: Stories of Stella, no doubt.

Anne: Diana . . .

Diana: I don't know how I thought you'd still wish to be friends with a country bumpkin like me once you'd . . . tasted the delights of town.

Anne: It's true that town offered many . . . tangy flavours, Diana. But in the end, I'd prefer the taste of country peach to any fruit town has to offer, no matter how waxed and gleaming.

Diana: Do you really mean that, Anne?

Anne: With all my heart, dearest. Ah, there are those dimples I've lain awake thinking of. My fuzzy little country peach . . .

Diana: It's a shame it's not the time of year for peaches. All we have are these preserves.

She hands Anne a bowl.

Diana: Mother finally let me do the canning this year. She felt that working with the peaches would keep my hands occupied.

Anne: Diana! These are never YOUR peaches? They're beautiful! Like congealed sunsets.

Diana: Are you going to try them or not?

Anne takes a bite of peaches.

Anne: Delicious. Better than Mrs. Lynde's.

Anne gets her whole face into the bowl of peaches and just gives 'er. Diana gets a little hot and bothered. When Anne's face emerges from the peach bowl . . .

Diana: Oh, Anne. Oh—you have some syrup . . .

Anne: Where?

Diana: Just here, on your . . .

They totally make out.

End scene.

Death

Betrayal

Dick

Rose: Of course, in all the novels of the time, romantic friends whose relationships went beyond Stage B: Linking Arms are separated from each other in one of three ways.

One of them dies; one of them horribly betrays the other; one or both of them succumb to the dick. I paraphrase Holt on that last point.

Which brings me to this question: Did the sexual relationships of romantic friends end when they married? After extensive literary research, I offer this chart. For those of you taking notes, the data is sorted according to the Hogan/Rathcourt research model.

Based on the evidence, I estimate that approximately 27% of romantic friends were, at one time or another, totally doing it.

Of that 27%:

5% remained old maids together doing it;

4% married but continued to do it;

4% married and ceased to do it but thought about it constantly instead of thinking of England;

14% "outgrew" the romantic friendship and later claimed they had just been "experimenting" after a crazy night of fiddle music and milk punch.

Early in the text, Montgomery gives us hope for Anne and Diana's continued exclusive relationship when Anne says to Marilla:

Hogan/Rathcourt Analysis

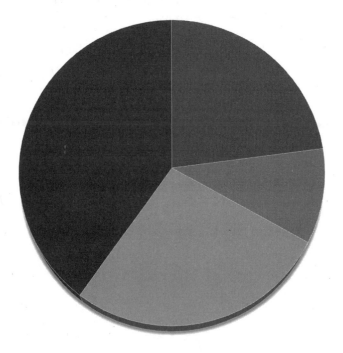

- Old Maids Doing It
- Married, But Still Doing It
- Married, Not Thinking of England
- Experimenting

"Diana and I are thinking seriously of promising each other that we will never marry but be nice old maids and live together forever."

A beautiful dream, but of course, it is not so. In this last scene, Diana, prevented from pursuing higher education and lacking Anne's imagination, is preparing to marry area man Fred Wright. On the night before her wedding, she shares her bed one last time with Anne.

SCENE THREE:

Diana: We're not really parting, Anne. I'm not going far away. We'll love each other just as much as ever. We've always kept that "oath" of . . . friendship we swore long ago, haven't we?

Anne: We've kept it faithfully, Diana. But things can't be quite the same after this. You'll have other interests. I'll just be on the outside.

Diana: You'll be inside my heart, Anne. You occupy a place there that Fred will never touch.

Anne: Oh, Diana.

They embrace.

Diana: Oh, Anne.

Anne: What is it, dearest?

Diana: Fred is a good man but . . . well . . . let us just say I suppose there are *other* places Fred will never touch either.

Anne: Then we must touch them all tonight, Diana. Every last one.

Diana: Aunt Josephine's sleeping in the spare room tonight. You know I'm a screamer, Anne. What if she hears us?

Anne: Well . . . what did we do last fall when your mother came into the kitchen while we were . . . dusting the shelves in the pantry? You were quiet as a mouse that time.

Diana: Silly Anne—I don't keep a corncob handy here in my room! Anymore.

Anne: Well, then you will just have to imagine it, Diana!

Anne jumps her.

End scene.

Rose: This scene marks Anne and Diana's final opportunity for girlish frolic. Anne goes back to university soon after and falls in love with tall, dark, handsome, boring Roy Gardner. The reader experiences a brief moment of hope that when Anne refuses Roy, she will then rush back to Avonlea, wrest Diana from Fred and elope with her to the States—but Montgomery, knowing her audience, will not risk alienating them with such a daring turn.

Instead, Anne ends up with childhood foe Gilbert Blythe, a young man whose own close relationship with Avonlea local Charlie Sloan makes one wonder if their eventual marriage and subsequent seven children were merely a marriage and seven children "of convenience."

One thing is clear—the rich tapestry of female relationships created by Montgomery allows us to view Anne and Diana in a new light—a light that reveals that they were totally doing it and Gilbert was just the beard.

Are there . . . any questions?

ROSEMARY ROWE is a playwright and performer whose plays, cabaret pieces, and occasional doughnut-sex fetish creations have been produced on stages across Canada. She is also the writer and co-creator of the award-winning lesbian web series *Seeking Simone* (tagline: Online dating has never been so gay!).

Rose is pretty sure *Anne of Green Gables* turned her gay, and thus her work tends to focus on corset-wearing lesbians in history, both real and "made up by Rose." In fact, for the 100th Anne-i-versary of *Anne of Green Gables*, Rose co-curated a sold-out cabaret called *Anne Made Me Gay: When Kindred Spirits Get Naked* at Buddies in Bad Times Theatre in Toronto.

Rose grew up in Edmonton, Alberta, where the streets are paved with gold! She's pretty sure she got her BFA in Theatre at York University but refuses to pay her TOTALLY BOGUS LIBRARY FINE to find out.

Rose keeps a personal blog, CreampuffRevolution.com, which landed her a spot as a national finalist on CBC Radio's Canada Writes '07 and has garnered her many nominations for real and imaginary Internet awards. She lives in Vancouver, BC, with her red-headed wife, Kate, and their junkyard dog, Emmy Lou.

The Confession
DARRIN M. MCCLOSKEY

I was told that when you go to confession you should remember to breathe.

↖ ↗ ↘

It was during the feast of St. Andrew. I had just returned to church—returned, yes, because it had been a long time—more than twenty years.

The sermon was about Jesus and his disciples. The priest read a passage from Matthew 22. He finished his homily with the words, "For many are called, but few are chosen." As the priest and his attendants filed out, he looked at me, shook his head, and then disappeared within the sacristy. I picked up the bible and read the passage again:

> But when the king came in to see the guests, he noticed a man there who was not wearing a wedding robe, and he said to him, "Friend, how did you get in here without a wedding robe?" And he was speechless. Then the king said to the attendants, "Bind him hand and foot, and throw him into the outer darkness, where there will be weeping and gnashing of teeth." For many are called, but few are chosen.

The altar lights went out and I suddenly realized I was grinding my teeth. But I was not weeping. I looked at how I was dressed. I was wearing nothing out of the ordinary, and there was nothing I could have added.

It must be him, I thought.

And so I went to confession.

ↂ ↗ ↘

"Father, why did you give me that look?"

"Son?"

"That look. After Mass yesterday, as you were leaving, you gave me this strange look."

"Son, this is a confessional, not a confrontational. Would you like to make a confession?"

"A confession? Uhh . . ."

"When was your last confession?"

"About twenty years ago."

"Twenty?"

"About that. Yes."

"Perhaps you should have made an appointment?"

"An appointment?"

"Yes."

"I can do that?"

"If it's necessary. And in your case I think it is."

"Wait—I just want to know why you gave me *that* look."

"*That* look? I'm not sure . . . "

"You remember, you gave me a strange look and then shook your head as if I weren't supposed to be in church—Wait. Why are you laughing?"

"I think it may be your conscience."

"My conscience?"

"It might be telling you something."

So I made an appointment.
Breathe.

↖ ↗ ↘

"Bless me, Father, for I have sinned. I confess to almighty God and to you, Father. It's been three days since my last confession."

"Three days? Son, that last visit was not a confession."

"No?"

"You confessed nothing."

"But I was in the confessional."

"Being in the confessional and confessing are two different things."

"Like going to a dance and not dancing."

"No, son, it's like going into a confessional and not confessing."

"Oh."

"So let's try again."

"Bless me, Father, for I have sinned. I confess to Almighty God and to you, Father. I have never ever confessed before."

"Never? But earlier you said . . ."

"I know, but I just realized I've never done a true confession before."

"Okay. Then let's get started."

"___"

"Son?"

"Yes."

"Do you have anything you'd like to confess?"

"Ummm . . ."

"Perhaps you need time to examine your conscience."

"Examine my conscience?"

"Yes. Take some time to go over your past and see where you have sinned."

"I can do that?"

"Yes, but not here." He pointed to the door.

And for two days I wept and gnashed my teeth.

Breathe.

ĸ ↗ ↘

"Bless me, Father, for I have sinned. I confess to Almighty God and to you, Father. I can't remember ever truly confessing."

"Continue."

"Okay, it's sex."

Sigh. "Again with the sex."

"What?"

"Never mind. Continue."

"Okay, I've had sex with men and enjoyed it. But I've had sex with women, and I've enjoyed that too, so I'm not really a homosexual. But I don't consider myself a heterosexual either. And I am not bisexual. Actually, I don't know what I am."

Breathe.

"And death. I think about suicide—a lot. But I'd never go through with it because I made a solemn promise to God many years ago that I would never take my own life—speculate on it, yes, and maybe toy with the idea, but I would never ever do it. So that's it. That's my confession."

"Is there anything else?"

"No, that's it. Just sex and death. That's really all I think about."

"Well, son, I don't know what to say. You really haven't confessed anything. It just sounds like you are just wrestling with things. Is there anything you want to confess?"

Breathe.

Breathe.

Breathe.

"Okay, wait, yes, back to sex. I've been in many relationships. And I am not proud of this. And now my hip."

"Your hip?"

"Yes, my hip. I have this gimpy walk now."

"Jacob."

"What?"

"Jacob, the son of Isaac, bad hip."

"Jacob?"

"Yes, Jacob wrestled with an angel. He won the match and he would not go away until he received the angel's blessing. But he suffered a gimpy hip ever since."

"But he got the blessing?"

"Yes."

"Then it was worth it."

"Yes."

"Can I have yours?"

"My hip?"

"No, your blessing."

"Are you finished?"

Breathe.

Breathe.

Breathe.

"Son?"

"Ummm . . . Wait, there it is again. *That look!* Why did you just give me that look?"

"Son? I think it may be your conscience."

And so I made another appointment.

Breathe.

DARRIN M. MCCLOSKEY began his writing adventure with a short four-hundred-word story published on Litbits.ca. Since then, he has had work published with *Melange Magazine, Bent,* and *Cezanne's Carrot.* He has also self-published one chapbook and two novellas: *Black Ice and other*

Solipsisms, Li'l Story: the true story of the rise and fall of the Great Canadian Novel, of which a continuation has just been published with The Toucan Magazine (online), along with *Tommy Taronta*—all appearing under Black Ice Press. He has had three pieces produced for the L&Q Cabaret. He has also recorded music under the pseudonym Steve Heron, which can be found at http://radio3.cbc.ca/#/bands/Steve-Heron. "The Confession" is an exaggerated account of some anxiety he experienced upon returning to the Catholic Church.

Whiter Than Snow

RUTH DYCKFEHDERAU

I am eleven years old. I know all about baptism. Every spring, my father fills the wheelbarrow with water and baptizes newborn puppies in it until they are dead. Well, he's joking—nobody *dies* from baptism. There's baptisms in our church all the time. Way back, when Stacey and I were six, we would sneak behind the pig barn on Sunday afternoons and play baptism with Barbie dolls in the deep puddle under the eavestrough. Only the Barbie dolls didn't die from baptism since they weren't alive to begin with. And they didn't have to wear any clothes because there weren't any boy dolls there. They were all, even the preacher doll, girls. Now that we're too old for dolls, Stacey and I take off our clothes and play baptism and stuff, just us, since there's always plenty of water and since there are no boys around. And nobody ever dies.

My Sunday school class is studying baptism. We're memorizing how serious it is. Old Mr. Siemens, whose leg sometimes rubs against mine during prayer, tells us and tells us in his cracked voice about the Relationship between God and Man. He takes us on a field trip out of our basement Sunday school room, past the teenager Sunday school rooms, past the adult Sunday school rooms, past the choir robe closet, and up the stairs to the Sanctuary. We've all been there lots of times before, but it looks different, hollow and ancient, when the pews have no people in them. We walk quietly down the centre red carpet past thirty-six rows of pews to the front where we climb the stage. Then Mr. Siemens moves the pulpit and shows us, hidden beneath the red carpet, sunken into the platform, the empty old falling-apart baptism tank. It's a small underground room, painted blue on the inside, with a drain at the bottom like a bathtub. There's a faded painting of an aimless river on the inside lid that becomes a background when the tank is open. Mr. Siemens steps down the three stairs into the tank and lies down on his back at the bottom so that we can all see it's big enough for even the tallest man to lie comfortably at rest beneath the still waters. I ask him about the rotting wood. My father says the wood around the tank is beginning to rot because water leaks into hidden places under the pulpit and platform every time the tank is full. Mr. Siemens says he doesn't know anything about that, but Stacey whispers to me that it's probably the sin in the water and not the water itself that's making the wood rot.

After he climbs out of the tank, Mr. Siemens takes us back to our classroom and turns on the overhead projector. He shows us a transparency with a bright-red heart on it, and a wet cloth. We look at the screen and watch Mr. Siemens wipe off the red and then we look at the cloth and see that the red is on the cloth now and not on the transparency. He says that baptism is like the cloth. It symbolizes making a man white, whiter than snow, so white that he won't even *want* to sin and dirty himself anymore. But I know it can't be the same for women, nothing in church is. My mother says girls are so dirty we could never be clean. I'm not too sure baptism works anyways. My father is a deacon and I've watched him empty the tank after other baptisms. I've never seen sin in that water. Mr. Siemens would say that's because baptism is a *symbolic* washing. But the water is real and wet, so you'd expect to see a little bit of sin anyways and you don't. The water is always just as clear after the baptism as it was before, though paint chips from the aimless river sometimes float in it. Except, of course, for the time the water was dirty after Peter Marantz was baptized, but he still smokes, even though he's saved, so what can you expect.

I don't really want to be baptized. No one else in my class is getting baptized yet. But I want my father to stop noticing that I am the only one in the family who is not baptized. And besides, it will make my mother proud and will be a kind of thank you for taking care of me when I am sick.

And so, with brand-new waterproof lip gloss, and with a snow-white dress for afterwards to symbolize that my bright red sin is washed away, I agree to be baptized that Sunday, the hottest day of summer, along with Jeremy, who is Stacey's older brother from the teenager Sunday school class, and five adult people. Wearing black robes with nothing but underwear underneath, we all sit on the very front bench, just beside the throbbing organ and the sanctuary fig plant. We look up at the cracked wooden cross at the front of the sanctuary and at the red carpet stage that is covered in plastic for today and we think about serious things.

The organ plays "Just as I Am Without One Plea" seven times, once for each of us. One at a time, as we are called, we walk the red plastic-covered carpet to the stage, then climb the three steps up the stage and the three steps down into the tank to where the minister waits for us standing in warm water up to his waist. He asks each of us, loudly, so everyone can hear, if we've been "Saved by the Blood of the Lamb" and if we "Declare Jesus Christ as our Personal Saviour." And we all say, loudly, "Yes I Do." And then he says that he baptizes us "In the Name of the Father, the Son, and the Holy Ghost," and then dunks us backwards under the water. Jeremy forgets to hold his nose and makes a loud spurting noise when his head goes under. Nobody in the whole church giggles even though it is very funny. When my turn comes, I hold my nose and say all the right things. And I see, on my way out of the tank, that the plastic has torn and the red carpet underneath is just soaked.

After we have changed out of the wet robes that cling like drenched fur, we are given Baptism Certificates and invited outside to the Baptismal Luncheon of open-faced sandwiches and runny red Jell-O. Jeremy and I, wearing our snow-white clothes, take our plates and Cokes down into the gully beside the church. We don't really say much while we eat. We've never really talked before and there doesn't seem to be much to say except to agree that baptism is very wet. After a while, we put the plates aside and Jeremy wonders when we will start feeling transformed. I tell him that only men feel transformed, that women really just keep on feeling wet. I keep on wishing he was Stacey. And, although I will not say this to Jeremy, I know that something has died deep, deep down inside me, that I wanted to feel transformed too. Despite everything my mother says about girls, I wanted to feel transformed.

Jeremy asks me if I've ever smoked. I shake my head no and say that smoking is Sin. And then I ask him to teach me. He reaches into his vest pocket, behind his watch on a chain, and pulls out his Baptism Certificate. He rips it and rolls some grass into it. Pretending it is lit, he shows me how to hold a cigarette and how to inhale, how to suck smoke just into my mouth and then breathe half smoke and half fresh air into my lungs. We sit in silence, puffing on a soggy pretend cigarette, listening to the choir rehearsing in the background for the Afternoon Service.

I saw one hanging on a tree

And then Jeremy says he'll show me something I've never seen. He gets on his knees, unzips his pants, and, in the shade of the huge willow, pulls out his thing.

In agony and blood

I am repulsed. It is unquestionably the ugliest part of a human body I have ever seen. It reminds me of uncooked sausage only more flexible. I would have thought it would be skin-coloured but in fact it is purple. And behind it is a soft-in-a-gross-way wrinkled thing hanging down. So wrinkled you would think it belonged on an old man's body.

He fixed his loving eyes on me

Jeremy begins to touch it, carefully, as if it is a sensitive object, easily hurt. It is all I can do to look at it, it is so ugly, but looking away is even harder. As he touches it, it begins to grow like a balloon being pumped full of water. And then I realize something important. I realize why adults have pubic hair. Well, I still don't know about women, but I'm pretty sure that men have pubic hair to cover these goblin tumours that stick out of their smooth bodies. If I was a man, I would grow *long* pubic hair.

As near his cross I stood.

He asks me to touch it. I tell him he is insane. I will never touch anything that looks like that, I would rather pick up soft dog doo with my fingers. He laughs and says my body is developing ahead of my brain.

Oh, can it be upon a tree my Saviour died for me?

We hear Mr. Siemens calling in the distance. The time has come to go inside, be congratulated, and take Holy Communion. We get up quickly and I spill some Jell-O on my dress. That's okay, it's down at the hem, nobody will notice. As I walk toward the church, Jeremy stuffs his swollen things back into his pants, yanks up the zipper, and runs after me like a white rabbit wearing a vest.

My soul is thrilled, my heart is filled, to think he died for me.

RUTH DYCKFEHDERAU is an Edmonton writer who has published in a variety of anthologies and literary journals, whose writing has been performed in Canada and Europe, and who is currently working on a novel. She teaches in the English and Film Studies Department at the University of Alberta and travels or works overseas as much as she possibly can. Ruth has had seven pieces performed at L&Q over the years, four of which have been published.

STANDupHOMO
(an excerpt)
NATHAN CUCKOW

*Darkness. A double-door closet stands stage right. The text **stand-up
homo** is projected on the closet doors. A voice is heard in the darkness.*

Voice: Are you ready? Twelve . . . eleven . . . ten . . . nine
. . . eight

Several other voices are heard overlapping one another.

Voice: Seven . . . six . . . five . . . four . . . three . . . two . . .
one

*A collage of noise builds to a climax. A laugh track is heard. Spotlight!
An effeminate man stands behind a microphone. He speaks with a
lisp. Beside him is a stool with a bottle of water sitting on it. Text is
projected on a giant closet standing stage right.*

Text: **the stand-up comedian**

Stand-Up: Nobody wants you to think that they're gay! I mean,
how do you think I feel? I'm performing in a show called
"STANDupHOMO"! And let me tell you, it's incredibly
hard performing in a show called "STANDupHOMO"
because as soon as I tell someone the title of my show,
the first thing they do is sit down! I'm serious. Down
they go. Like a skydiver whose parachute didn't open!
"Oh my God, I'm going to hit the ground, but I don't

care as long as no one thinks that I'm gay—SPLAT!" They don't care. They hear the word STAND and the word HOMO and they can't hit the ground quick enough! Good thing you're all sitting down right now, or I just might think . . . What people don't realize is that the HOMO in STANDupHOMO is actually HOMO as in HOMOSAPIEN. Not homosexual! It's kind of embarrassing. I say STANDupHOMO and all of a sudden it's a competition to see who is the last one standing. Usually it's me. Why is that? Anyway, that's not important. What is important is that before I go any further, I mean, if nobody minds, I'd really like to, uh, to . . . tell you a secret? I mean, I know we really don't know each other that well yet, well I guess I do see some familiar faces—Mom. Dad. I'm just kidding! I just pointed at two men! . . . Like I'd invite my parents to a show called "STANDupHOMO," starring me, their son. What do you think I am—retarded? Just so you know, when I say that something is "retarded" I'm not saying that I think it's "mentally challenged." I'm saying that I think it's gay! Not like gay-homosexual, but like stupid-gay. Not stoopid, like s-t-o-o-p-i-d, you know, like cool-gay, but stupid, s-t-u-p-i-d, like dumb-gay. Not homosexual-gay, not retarded-gay, but dumb gay. But the point being, I'm not trying to insult anyone here. These are just words I was taught through my childhood, and I know it's not okay to use these words anymore, well unless of course you are gay, or mentally challenged, whatever, because then it's like you are reclaiming the word so people can't use it against you, you know what I mean? Like when black people say, "My nigga!" Or the homosexuals say, "My faggot." . . . Funny, you never hear mentally challenged people call each other "My retard." Anyway, what I'm trying to say here is that these are just words that have been ingrained into my brain and at the most inappropriate moments, out they come. So my apologies to any small retarded children there might be in the audience. Or any parents of small retarded children. Or any small children whose parents are black, gay, and retarded.

My therapist says it's important for me to apologize if I've offended someone. She says—

Text: **the therapist**

Therapist: You are displaying classic passive-aggressive behaviour patterns.

Stand-Up: But I just say to her, "Fine. Whatever. Think what you want." She's a fucking idiot! It is not my intention to offend anyone. Honestly. I think that all people should be treated with tolerance, kindness, and compassion. Because, we're all the same, you know what I mean? We're all just people. We all eat, sleep, shit, piss, fuck. Some people piss and shit on the people they fuck! It's true. It's so very true.

Text: **we are all the same**

Stand-Up: Now I'm not saying that people can't be individuals. All I'm saying is that we're human beings first, so before we are different from each other, we're all the same. Except for the niggers and the Jews . . . I'm just kidding, certainly I am just kidding about that! Some of my best friends are Jews. Well, not some of them, but one is. I don't have any black friends, but I fully love the rap music. But I digress. *(He takes a deep breath.)* Yes. Right.

Text: **my secret**

Stand-Up: This is really hard for me to say. You see, I am a . . . uh . . . I just think that it's really important before you get to know me any better that I just come right out and tell you the truth. *(He clears his throat and takes another breath.)* I am . . . I'm a . . . I'm a Mormon!

Text: **the church of jesus christ of the latter day saints**

Stand-Up: There, I said it. I'm Mormon! You know the Church of Jesus Christ of the Latter Day Saints? They have those commercials? I'm a Mormon, and I'm not ashamed. I mean, there's lots of really positive things about my church, like we promote the importance of family values, and that you should try to live your life like Jesus did. To do unto others as would you . . . no . . . do unto others as do you unto . . . no . . . do unto . . . oh however the fuck it goes! I'm a Mormon. And no I don't have more than one wife. I mean, sometimes I might wish I did. Just imagine all that holy poontang! But yet again, I digress. I am a Mormon. *(He takes a deep breath.)* And no, I'm not a homosexual.

Text: **persona**

Therapist: "Persona." The role that one assumes or displays in society; one's public image or personality, as distinguished from the inner self.

Text: **are you that way?**

Stand-Up: Because I can tell a lot of you are thinking that I am, you know, *that way*. I know people always assume that I'm *that way* because I talk with a lisp. Which I know is associated with the gay voice, you know, how gay people just talk with that voice, that sounds so, you know . . . gay. But I mean, gay people choose to talk like that, I was born this way! I mean, I've tried rehabilitation, but there's absolutely nothing I can do to control it! Seriously, I suffer from a sibilant *S*. It's not an excuse. And, I mean, it's not like I want to go on about it, but, man, do I-ever-love-pussy! I mean, I just can't get enough of it. Seriously. I may not sound like it, but I am one pussy-loving kind of man. And it's hard, you know? Like when I meet an attractive girl, she sees me, she thinks, Oh, he looks like such a nice guy, and then I open my mouth, and all of a sudden I turn into this nasty little cocksucker because I talk with a lisp! I like to take it in the face because I have "issues" with my "ssssss!" It's such a sexual stereotype!

Text: **alter-persona**

Therapist: Each Alter-persona is designed to perform a specific function. They are endowed with characteristic traits that the Original Personality would have taken on, if it were in charge. The situation, perhaps, could be viewed as the operating of a doll making factory, but only the outfits of clothing are being produced. The doll, itself, is not present.

Stand-Up: Not that it matters if people think that I'm gay. I think gay people are great. Some of my best friends are gay. I just want everyone here to know for the record that I am not. Gay. Not that it matters. I'm okay with gay. Gay is great!

Text: **love the sinner, but hate the sin**

Stand-Up: Being gay is not okay for the Mormons. Mormons, like most religions, believe that homosexuality is wrong, but I just prefer to "Love the sinner, but hate the sin." So, for example, I *love* Ellen Degeneres, I just *hate* the fact that she eats pussy. Because that's my job! Now, I used to hate Anne Heche, for letting Ellen, you know? But now Anne only has men munch on her muffin, so she's okay! Not that I have a problem with lesbians. "Love the sinner, but hate the sin." I even took the time to read their book, *women are from venus, women are from venus*!

Text: **women are from venus, women are from venus**

Stand-Up: Anybody else read that? The title is written in lower case letters so everyone knows that lesbians are also postmodern feminists!

Text: **gaydar**

Stand-Up: My gay best friend Bruce said to me, "You've got good 'gaydar.' And I said, "What's gaydar?" and he said, "It's a radar that detects gay people, you spazz!" And apparently it's incredibly rare for straight men to have this ability, but I guess it's like I was born with a gay sixth sense. *(Whispered reference to the movie* The Sixth Sense.*)* "I see gay people . . . all around me."

Text: **half-gay**

Stand-Up: Actually, my gay best friend Bruce isn't actually gay. He's bisexual, but he doesn't like saying that he's bisexual because he thinks it makes him sound too promiscuous, you know? "Oh, I'm bisexual. I have sex with men AND women. I fuck this! I fuck that! Oh, you got one of those? Here, stick it in me!"

Instead he prefers to be called "Half-Gay" because he insists he's only gay half of the time. I asked Bruce, "Which half?" He said, "The bottom half, of course!"

He goes to the stool beside him and opens the bottle of water.

Man, am I ever thirsty. *(He takes a sip.)* Mmm, it's delicious! *(He takes another sip.)* Mmm. So good! *(He takes another sip.)* Mmm! It's vodka.

He returns to the microphone.

Okay then, like I was saying, I'm not a homosexual, but I totally love the gays. Well, except the gays who are dumb. Then it's like, "You are so *gay* and also you're totally gay!"

Text: **the princess**

Princess: *(She smokes an imaginary cigarette.)* Why is it when a woman stands up for herself she's considered a bitch, and yet if a man does, he's considered a man? Men are expected to stand up for themselves. If they don't, other men will say that they have no "balls" or call them a name that associates them with being a woman. Ironically, I never learned how to stand up for myself until I stopped being a man and became a woman.

Text: **he's a boy but he wears a dress**

Princess: I was given the name Princess in the sixth grade when I showed up to school wearing my mother's red dress. My teacher, Ms. Milner, sent me home to change into something more suitable for a young man to wear, and as I was leaving the classroom the other students started chanting—

Children: "Princess, Princess, he's a boy, but he wears a dress!"

Princess: I didn't care. I found the name to be rather appropriate. Besides, they could have called me anything and it wouldn't have mattered. I was wearing my mother's red dress and none of those little fuckers could take that away from me. *(She takes a drag.)* Did I mention that I hate children? Well I do, and I'm so very glad that I can't actually reproduce because if I did ever have a child, I'd be forced to drown it in the North Saskatchewan River. What? Even though I lack female reproductive organs, I can still be a cunt!

NATHAN CUCKOW is an award-winning, Edmonton-based actor, producer, and playwright and is the co-artistic director of Edmonton's critically acclaimed independent theatre company Kill Your Television. His plays have been commissioned and produced locally in Edmonton by Northern Light Theatre (*3 Different Heavens*) and Azimuth Theatre (*3 . . . 2 . . . 1*, co-written with Chris Craddock and published by Signature Editions in the collection *Two Hands Clapping*), and have been presented across Canada as well as internationally in Dublin, Ireland, and New York City, where his musical, *BASH'd!* (co-written with Chris Craddock) ran for three months Off-Broadway. *BASH'd!* continues to tour and was recently published by Talonbooks. He is the proud recipient of a GLAAD Media Award for Outstanding New York Theatre and six Sterling Awards, including Outstanding Performance by an Actor in a Leading Role, for his performance in Kill Your Television's production of Daniel MacIvor's one-man show *Monster*.

Touring and Scoring:
Tales of a Lesbian Stand-Up Comic
SUSAN JEREMY

THE MANAGER — ALBANY, NEW YORK 1987

We went out after the show. Me (I'm the middle act), the emcee, the headliner, the cook, and the manager. This is the way it always is when you're playing a comedy club in a non-eventful town. Usually, it's me and the guys. But at this club, Giggles, in Albany, the manager is an attractive, semi-tough blonde who barks orders at her staff like she could handle anything thrown at her. At least that's how she presented herself. We're at the local drinking hole. It's crowded and smoky.

The headliner is an overweight coke-driven guy who is used to scoring any drunk waitress. He's working the shot-girl in the cowgirl outfit. She is impressed that he is from NY—that's how he hooks them. The emcee is trying to be funny, but no one is having it because he's not funny. The cook is a hairy guy with a bad complexion. Years of cooking fried zucchini sticks.

The manager hands me a beer. "Here. I bought this for you because I like your smile."

Is she flirting with me? We are in a straight bar in Dumbfuck. The other comics are here. It's pre-*Ellen*, pre-*Will & Grace*. Comics don't get on TV shows unless they appear straight. That's what I do on the road: let the guys flirt with me while I fantasize about the girls—and compete with the headliners who always take the waitresses. Unless

I'm the headliner—then I retreat to my hotel room because the other comics start working me. Or the booker, usually an Italian guy named Vinny who can't believe the girl comic is not only funny but hot. Yeah, I wear tight jeans, I have high boots. I have long blond, very un-lesbian hair. (I grew up in Long Island. It's a symptom of my upbringing.)

I look at the manager. She has an attractive toughness, in a Jodi Foster way. I take the beer and another and another. Some guy asks me to dance. I go to the sawdust dance floor with him while the manager looks on. My fantasies need a break. She's in charge of my paycheque. I have to play it cool.

ㅤㅤㅤㅤㅤㅤㅤ↖ ↗ ↘

It's later that night . . . the bar's emptied out. We closed it. Me, the cook, and the manager. The emcee went home hours ago . . . no one would laugh at his jokes. The headliner either left with the cowgirl or passed out or both. The cook is now working me, like he stands a chance. I'm the centre of attention.

The manager is still flirting and saying things like, "So how did you get to be so entertaining, so sexy?"

She is making me nervous. I'm not in my element. This is my bread-and-butter gig.

"Let's go," she says to me and the cook. Always the manager; still calling the shots. We pile into her small green truck with a lawnmower in the back. I'm in the middle. She handles the clutch like a pro. The cook suggests we smoke a joint at his house. He's thinking ménage. She stops him in mid-pitch.

"No thanks, I have to get up early tomorrow, I'll drop you off."

The cook points out that he's the second stop because we'll pass my hotel first. She misses the turn. "Oops . . . I guess you're the first stop." She smiles at me coyly . . . I say nothing. I can't believe how this is unfolding.

We arrive at the cook's house. He makes one last attempt: "It's really good pot."

"See ya!" she calls as she peels out of his driveway.

Now it's just me. And her. Silent. Driving back to my hotel. I'm still not sure. I could be reading this wrong. I'm letting her make the move. She stops in the parking lot of the Red Roof Inn. Motor still running. I get out.

"Thanks for the ride," I say, ever-so cool.

She reaches in the backseat and pulls out a half bottle of red wine. "Can I come in and finish this?"

I smile. This is going to happen! We go to my room. Second floor, next to the ice machine. I put on the TV and sit on the bed. I'm drunk and very horny. She sits next to me and kisses me. AH HAH! She made the first move—anything goes now. I kiss her back, deeply. She starts to take my shirt off. I'm peeling hers off. Bras fly off, skin to skin . . . nipple to nipple. My hands move to her thigh. She pulls away.

"I'm not a lesbian."

"Neither am I," I lie. I kiss her again. She responds, then stops abruptly.

"NO, really. I'm not."

She jumps up, puts on her shirt. She runs out, leaving skid marks in the carpet. Her bra left on the floor.

↖   ↗   ↘

The next night I have to return to the club for my last show, to get paid. I carry a small plastic bag with her bra inside it. She greets me from across the bar.

"Hi, Susan!"

A way-too-happy greeting.

I say, "Hey" to no one in particular and toss the plastic bag at her without looking up. I proceed to the green room.

NICE CAR

Her hand is on my thigh. I'm wet. Her breasts are perfect. I could see their shape through her white T-shirt. She's so interesting. She tells me of her days as a photographer in Saudi Arabia, of her mother dying of cancer. Her life in the army. It all seems like so much . . . she's only twenty-five. How could she have done all this? I doubt her story, but I can't pull my eyes from her long black hair brushing over her shoulder.

What is she doing in this bar at 1:00 AM on a Monday night? I question my instincts . . . surely not an axe murderer, maybe a psychiatric patient. Big deal. I'm used to that from my ex-girlfriend. So what's a little personality disorder . . . she's a babe. I know it, the bartender knows it, and there's no one else in the bar except the overweight couple slow dancing to Gloria Estefan. Perhaps she's just lonely . . . that's why I'm here. Three weeks on the road, a beautiful room at the Hilton. Miami: a city alive—but not on a Monday night in the early 1990s. I found the only lesbian bar. A Latin dive. But it was open and there was an extraordinary car in the front. A black race car with sleek windows. When I sat at the bar it was natural to sit near her—she was the only one there. But God did I luck out.

Now she is leaning toward me, whispering.

SHE: "Let's go."

I'm still a little hesitant. I have cash in the hotel room. "Another drink?"

SHE: "I can't . . . I'm on a lude."

Oh, drugs . . . I hate drugs. But she is so . . . *so* what I want right now. Her perfect lips continue to move while she asks if I'll do her a favour. "It depends," I say, while my hand equally caresses her thigh.

SHE: "Just follow me in your car. I have to drop this car off."

"Did you borrow it?"

SHE: "Sort of . . . "

I'm confused. "Well, do you know the person that you sort of borrowed the car from?" She starts to giggle.

SHE: "Well, no."

ALARM! DISAPPOINTMENT! "So you stole it?"

SHE: "I hate that word—*stole*."

She tries to kiss me, her hand now rubbing my zipper.

"I have to leave," I say, pulling her hand off of me. "Alone!"

Dammit, why me?? Why do I always attract the dangerous ones, the ex-cons, the Geminis??

In the parking lot, I stop to admire the Jaguar. I touch it and get wetter.

THE MODEL
She was six-foot-one, her name: Natasha. We left the bar at 2:00 AM on a Tuesday. "Whose place, mine or yours," I asked (quite drunk).

SHE: "Where do you live?"

Thompson Street.

SHE: "Me too."

Oh my God this stunning creature lives on my block and I never saw her? Manhattan can be like that. A city of fabulous strangers living in anonymity.

What number?

SHE: "75."

210.

SHE: "Your place."

So off we went. Walking/stumbling/hanging on each other, knowing that we would be naked soon. Two drunk strangers who met with the same plan: sex on a Tuesday. Obviously neither of us kept morning hours. Writhing bodies on the floor, bed, against the wall. Over the chair. There was not one inch of the room that we didn't fuck in. It looked like I was robbed afterwards. Clothes and furniture everywhere . . . the walls still trembling the next day. I slept exhausted, delighted, spinning from the tequila. When I woke up she was gone. Just the faint smell of her perfume remained.

Two weeks later when thumbing through a back issue of *Vogue*, there she was. In a wild dress with a menacing look.

I knew that look. The ad was for a perfume. Tigress.

I immediately went out and bought it.

SUSAN JEREMY is a solo performer and playwright in New York City. She is the co-author of four one-person plays dealing with everything from a fast-paced memoir to a crazy green card wedding. She wishes to thank her director and writing partner, Mary Fulham, for all her structure and skill. Susan went from being an accomplished stand-up comic touring the United States and Canada to teaching kids with special needs and is currently writing a book entitled *Tales of a Traveling Teacher*. She is also the author of numerous short comical pieces, one of which was published in the Edinburgh *Scotsman*, the others on Internet blogs and in local weekly papers.

Chicken Mom
NICK GREEN

Brenda is standing against the kitchen counter, smoking. On the counter rests a hardcover book and an ashtray. Though we never actually hear it, throughout the monologue her son, Daniel, is calling her from the basement, which is why she keeps covering her ears.

Brenda: A chicken and an egg are lying in bed. The chicken is leaning against the headboard, smoking a cigarette with a satisfied smile. The egg, looking a bit ticked off, grabs the sheet, rolls over, and says, "Well, I guess we finally answered THAT question!"

What a filthy joke! Horrible.

Why did the chicken cross the road? To get away from her son and husband.

Laughs.

It says, in the book, I should understand that "by distancing myself from my child, I may be causing severe damage." Well, poop. I'm taking a different course of action. I have been inspired elsewhere Ms. Dr. Griffiths-Rock.

There is, after all, an awful lot to learn. Yes. There is a lot to learn from chickens.

Hens, actually. Not roosters as much. A little. Mostly from hens.

Why did the hen cross the road? She probably brought her son with her. Dragged him. Dumb little bitch.

I was reading this book. It's of the self-help variety. There were many on this subject matter. I spent a full three-quarters of an hour just studying the cover of each book. I finally settled on this one because the chapter division seemed the most practical, and the author looked very credible. Turns out, I don't think she has a clue what she is talking about.

It says here to be outspoken and vocal in order to "instill in your child a sense of confidence and safety." Sounds like it makes sense, doesn't it? Once, I would have believed that too, but now, no. I am fed up and my hen logic teaches me better than that.

She puts her hands to her ears and shakes her head.

Right. You're wondering . . . this isn't just any parenting book. No-ho-ho, this is *Colourful Parenting; Raising a Rainbow,* by Dr. Adele Griffiths-Rock. I should have caught on by the name alone. I was fooled by the fact that she's so credible looking. Damn women who wear square-framed glasses. They just look like good mothers and doctors, don't they?

In case you didn't catch it, the book is about raising a gay teenager. My son is gay. I have a gay son. Gay gay. Really gay. He's sixteen, Daniel, and he is a pain in the ass.

Oh, I shouldn't say that. Hoo, I'm being rash. I'm just frustrated. I'm just having a hard time adjusting to my new psychology. I'm having a hard time dealing with the fact that I seem to HATE MY CHILD sometimes, which is why I'm purposely neglecting him.

No. No. I'm purposely neglecting him because I love him.

Chickens have this phase called "going broody" where they will sit in their nests and barely move while they incubate their eggs. They rarely leave to even pee or eat or dust bathe. They just sit there and turn their eggs so the yolk doesn't stick to the side of the shell. Going broody. Sounds like moody, which some people have said that I am, but chickens aren't so that's not relevant. That's just judgmental.

For the first fourteen years of Daniel's life, you could say I was "going broody." Obviously I left the house and ate and bathed, but for the most part I stayed home and nurtured my son. This isn't complaining. I was happy, Doug, my husband, was happy to bring home the bacon, and Daniel was happy in my arms. I imagine what it's like for these hens, it wasn't even a choice but an instinct.

And what a child! What a golden egg. We went every-where together. Doug would come home at night and we would have these family dinners. Daniel would talk and talk and talk, and Doug and I would just listen. I guess he was different. Of course he was different, that's why we got along. I understand . . . understood him. Unlike other kids, he begged to go shopping with me. It seemed to be his favourite pastime. He would be furious if I ever entered a Linens 'n Things without him. And *oh* the help in the garden!

I suppose I should have been a bit more aware of how often he wore my shoes around the house. And how he would constantly complain about how Jem doll clothes wouldn't fit Barbie. But I just smiled. I didn't try to change him. Why should I? He was so cute and it made him happy. Doug thought it was just a phase, which is cliché to the point of nausea. Not that it bothered Doug either. I have no idea what bothers him now, locked away in that attic. Daniel locked away in that basement. My men. Locking themselves away.

Daniel did so well in school, except for gym. And math. And science. And French, actually. But he was a solid B student in English and he got an A in art in grade six.

The house was happy and peaceful, warm and lovely. Broody. It was broody. And moody if we're going to be honest, but why be judgmental?

Then at fourteen, things began to change around the nest. My chick, my Daniel, started darkening away from me. Slowly at first, but within a few months everything had changed. He started staying out later and later. I never gave him a real curfew because I always knew where he was, and Doug was very against it. Not anymore. His friends, he used to have such nice friends whom he'd known all his life. Suddenly he's hanging out with this angry-looking boy with a spike through his lower lip and a girl with a bald head who would appear in my living room with a cat, wearing a leash, on her shoulder. He starts wearing a lot of black, he dyes his hair. He wore more vinyl than a shower curtain. And he stopped seeing all his other good childhood friends, except Cameron, our neighbour.

She pauses, covers ears.

Dr. Griffiths-Rock called this his "gothic" stage, apparently very common with gay teens. I didn't have the book back then, but in retrospect it makes sense. She said that a teen's sexual confusion will often turn them to a fascination with dark thoughts, and that it usually isn't as serious as it seems.

I never took it that seriously, the dark stuff. He wants to be a vampire? Well, I guess I just hope he's a nice vampire who doesn't do drugs and washes his hands. I never spoke to him about it. Guess I was chicken. Doug wasn't scared. He just seemed to be at a loss for words. That's what he does. Gets lost.

You know who says a lot about chickens? Aesop. The thing is, in his tales the chickens are always about to be eaten. They're always dinner.

Last year. It was hard up until then, but then there was last year. Last year, he "came out of the closet" to me and Doug. Came out of the closet. Such a funny term. If you could only see Daniel's closet. There isn't enough room in there for another pair of shoes, much less a sexually confused teenager. I guess you have to be a mother to really appreciate that. Well . . . last year, in the fall of last year right after the first week of school, Daniel sat us down and very coolly informed us that he is a homosexual. He said gay, not homosexual, but he didn't seem very happy to me.

It was all I could do not to just shriek, "Well . . . DUH!" but I didn't. I'm sure there's something scientific saying that a boy doesn't know until a certain age or other, but I've always had a feeling.

All right, I know I have made myself out to be quite the hip, tolerant parent. I'll admit that I did a bit of pulling.

I tried to pull him in a different direction . . . just a little bit. Doug and I put him into soccer. At first he was into it because he really liked the shoes. The novelty quickly wore off and he was soon butting heads with the evil little boys on his team. I mean, just rotten little shits. I'd have thrown each of them down a flight of stairs, one by one, if I could have.

You find that shocking? I'll tell you what's shocking. The words that parents allow their children to say. The names they allow their children to call. The intolerant and ridiculously privileged, self-entitled, CRUEL attitude they pass to their cruel, self-entitled, ridiculously privileged, intolerant children. That is shocking.

Cameron, our neighbour, stood up for Daniel a lot, but it was too much and Daniel quit soccer. Then he wanted to go into ballet so I put him into baseball.

I don't know if he resents me for all this. I think he gets it.

She covers her ears and hums to herself.

The chicken didn't cross that road. The road crossed that chicken.

So he told us and I smiled and grabbed his hand, but before I could say anything, he rolled his eyes and went downstairs to his room. Starting the year of the invisible son, which exists to this day.

I wanted to talk about it with Doug, but he just flew off to his coffee shop to do God-only knows. Smoke pot with a seventeen-year-old? He thinks I don't know. He looked me in the eye, then left the room.

Dinners were unbearable. Our dinners were once triumphant. Now they hurt as Daniel sulked and Doug stared off in the distance.

And thus began the year of "Colourful Parenting" and that know-it-all bitch, Dr. Adele Griffiths-Rock. I was trying to keep the relationship "in many supportive rainbow spectrums," by respecting his "purple and indigo days" and celebrating the "red, orange, and yellow" days. It never said what to do on "green" days, which I'm assuming were the days he was sick, so I just gave him chicken soup.

Those goddamned square-framed glasses! She looked so credible.

I also became involved! I joined PFLAG! I'd been going to meetings for the last ten months, almost a year. I was actually moving up in the pecking order, especially because I always bought really good scones for the meetings. But then, last week—

I thought I was going in the right direction. There was this image in my head of going broody for another fourteen years. Warmth.

Then last week I was there setting up for a meeting when Daniel walked in with that little bald—girl friend of his, she calls herself Krsh, which has no vowel in it, so I don't see how she can call that a name. They walked up to me, Krsh leading the way, Daniel trailing behind, staring at the ground. Krsh looked me in the face and told me . . . she *informed* me that I was neither a friend nor much of a parent to Daniel, so I didn't really "have any business being a part of PFLAG."

And I can't even speak. I can't even shake my head or nod or react to this little girl, speaking on behalf of my drowning son. I looked at him.

"Is this true, Daniel?"

"Do you feel this way, Daniel?"

Tears fill her eyes.

"Do you want me to leave, Daniel?"

He just stands there, staring at the ground. There was something in his eye. A hurt. A swirling something dark hurt. One that made his vision short. A pain that made him unable to see beyond himself.

He shrugged. He nodded.

I put down the tray of vegan brownies that I had made, I grabbed my purse, and I walked out the door.

Sometimes I wish we were allowed just one free shot at our child. One social-services free shot to the back of the head. It'd be even better if the kid knew about it, but didn't know when it was coming.

Child abuse is not funny. I would never hit my child. It's just that this was never covered in my book.

Why did the chicken cross the road? There is no other side. It's just the same street with another road and another street across from it.

About three days ago, I realized there wasn't much to that book at all. I began to wonder what authority this credible-looking woman had when it came to having gay children. This was her experience when it came to raising one. But she had never experienced being me, in my situation, or actually being a gay teen. And then I realized . . . *NEITHER HAVE I!* What the hell am I doing? He's trying to figure this out, and I'm working on him like a lab experiment. So then I began to think about the hens.

Seems like a bit of a jump, doesn't it? I remember hearing somewhere that one should never help a chick out of its egg. The stages of an egg hatching are complex and delicate, so you could kill the chick if you try removing the eggshell. It's also psychological. The struggle of getting out of the egg is integral to giving the chick coping and survival skills. Hens never help their chick out of the egg. It's in nature's design.

Sometimes you just need to shut up and let things sort themselves out.

All this time I have being pulling at your pieces of shell, impatient to let you come out of it yourself, just pulling and pulling and pulling. But, Daniel, I don't mean to pull you down. My pulling isn't supposed to be a tug-of-war. It's supposed to be a pulley. I pull down so that you can go up. See, I didn't know that my chick can fly on his own.

No more book. I'm giving up on you. I'm doing the chicken. Not mother hen . . . there's too much pecking and picking. No. I'm going to be the chicken mother.

Pick your shells off, and I'll ignore you until you do. Even if it kills me, and if you call for me one more time I think my heart might break and I might pull out all my hair. I will ignore you and let you figure this out. But you'd better believe that the minute you're out of all your shell, it's right back under the wing with you.

Why did the chicken cross the road? So the chick would know to follow.

Lights fade out.

NICK GREEN is an award-winning playwright and professional actor, and is really excited to be a part of this anthology! Previous writing credits include *Undercovered* (Exposure Queer Arts and Cultural Festival), *Left Field* (Concrete Theatre), *Kenny Timeless* (8-0-8 Productions), *Darling I Hate You, In the Margins*, and *Sounds of Rain* (Loud & Queer), *GayFace* (Mischief and Mayhem), *2 Queens & A Joker*, and *Triple Platinum* (Guys in Disguise, co-written with Trevor Schmidt and Darrin Hagen), and his Sterling Award-winning *Coffee Dad, Chicken Mom and the Fabulous Buddha Boi* (Guy UnDisguised/Edmonton Fringe Festival/New York's Frigid Festival). Nick is also the resident playwright for Twenties Street Productions in Fort Edmonton Park, for which he has written *Blue Heaven, Under the Big Top, A Long Night, Love Letters,* and *The Curse of Pigeon Lake.* Nick is a graduate of the University of Alberta's BFA Acting Program.

for theodore

LAURIE MACFAYDEN

i don't know who they're burying here tonight,
but it sure as hell isn't our friend ted.
our friend ted was a maverick, a clown, a bullshitter, an outlaw,
a soothsayer, a freckled, red-haired, gentle gem of a man.

that guy they're burying here tonight is a clean-cut shell,
some sort of sanitized, one-dimensional, god-fearing mannequin.

if you didn't know ted, you'd swear
from what that lunatic preacher's saying
that he was some kind of saint
who did nothing but worship his family and walk with the lord.

our friend teddy was no saint. he had a bit of the devil in him, in
    fact.
and excuse me, mister preacher, with the brandy on your breath,
but the teddy we knew and loved had absolutely no relationship
to the lord of whom you speak. oh, teddy took long walks,
but not with the lord. he walked with angels, to be sure,
but not the kind you're invoking now.
teddy walked with his dogs through mackenzie ravine, but he also
walked with the homeless, the drunken, the downtrodden, the
    slightly-this-side-of crazy.

yeah, our ted was a bit weird.
so how come we're hearing none of that at his funeral?
all we're hearing about is his alleged faith—
and god, this preacher is taking liberties. ted had faith, all right:
faith in campfires, in cheap beer, in hot dogs and cigarettes
and '70s ballad rock. faith in fish and ravens and plain-looking
women in polka-dot dresses. faith in levi's jeans and sturdy boots
and christmas ornaments and firecrackers. but he had no time
for faith in the fire-and-brimstone god you keep insisting was
   constantly by his side.

no, our ted didn't walk with that lord.
and you can go straight to hell, mister preacher, for suggesting that
   he did.
our friend ted talked with tree spirits and with his dead grandmother.
he walked with dan, his lover of 14 years
—how come you're not mentioning that?

he walked to the corner for flavoured coffee and pop rocks
and pepperoni sticks. he walked with a swagger and a grin
and sometimes with a bit of a flounce . . .
but he did not walk with your lord god father, mister preacher,
and shame on you for trying to suggest that he did.
shame on you for lying about our friend ted.

teddy was no saint. teddy had flaws. hell, we all do.
we are all teetering on the edge of brokenness;
we all have our trips in and out of the darkness.
our teddy survived a childhood of poverty and neglect and abuse.
who could blame him for occasionally hearing voices
and taking road trips with other fallen angels?

our friend teddy never made a marriage vow, but he made art.
he made curtains. he made a mean lasagna. he made a loving home,
and he made an honest buck.

teddy made a nativity scene out of real wood for his front yard—
and he wept when the neighbourhood kids destroyed it.
they kicked it down and pissed on it, and teddy wept
because even though he was not particularly religious,
he'd wanted to make something nice for christmas,
for the neighbourhood . . . and the neighbourhood let him down.

our teddy drank gin and smoked. he never took a wife
and he never went to church. he was a real person
made of real flesh and blood—not some christly cardboard cutout
living for the day he would go to be with someone else's lord.

thunder & jesus, mister preacher, i don't know what particular
abomination you're burying here tonight, but it sure as hell
isn't our friend teddy. the teddy you're describing never existed.

but the funny thing is, he'd probably forgive you
for telling all of these lies. that's the kind of guy he was:
a seriously flawed, forgiving, huge-hearted sweet faggot of a guy.

we miss him dearly.

LAURIE MACFAYDEN is a former Edmonton sports journalist who left the news media in 2007 to concentrate on her own writing and painting. Her debut collection of poems, *White Shirt* ("a bust-out-of-the-closet voice" published 2010) was long-listed for the Alberta Readers Choice Awards, shortlisted for the Lambda Literary Awards, and winner of the 2011 Gold Crown Literary Society Award for lesbian poetry. She performed in Fairy Tales & Swallow-A-Bicycle's inaugural Queer Arts & Culture Festival (2011) and is a frequent reader on the Raving Poets' open-mic stage in Edmonton. Her writing has appeared in *The New Quarterly* literary journal; Spire Poetry Poster; the Ontario Poetry Society's anthology *Love: The Main Course*; and at DailyHaiku. org. Several of her pieces, including "Those of Us," "Homo for the Holidays," and "The L-Word: Nothing to Wear to the Dinah," have been performed at Edmonton's annual Loud & Queer Cabaret. Her art lives at lauriemacfayden.com.

Traffic
NORM SACUTA

EDMONTON, MAY 2006

The series has been tied!
And Her Most Royal Imperial Sovereign of the Wild Rose,
Weena Love, awaits the light change. Downtown
reasonable, yet dressy, a hiked skirt,
spiked heels and oriental eye paint, a chiffon blouse
tight over big ones that rest beneath her fox stole.
She waves and waves as a born-againer might
so happy at this opportunity from the Lord. Each happy horn
a kiss blown, a wink thrown as if
she were every goal ever scored.

The traffic, honking, delirious, banner-filled and fluid,
is uncertain what to do with all this freedom
of movement. Whyte is so stagnant with danger,
drunken boys in ball caps
aching fists and fires set at every intersection.
And so families, afraid, drive to Jasper
in SUVs and pickups, pass this single gay block with the bar above
and Weena below, in traffic.

The light turns red and she walks halfway
across the intersection, faces the first pickup and wiggles

toward the hood, her heels make her high
enough to sit back and sprawl, the teeter-tottered
motion of fox between her legs, she ends
with kisses against the windshield, the two
men hoot through the open window, pinch her ass,
oblivious yet thankful for so much.

But Weena is no one-truck woman;
she's off as if at Walmart, fingers touching
opposite aisles as she walks the dividing line between lanes.
There's a boy of 10, his Oilers banner a stick, she
bends away with her tight wide ass
rounded from those stilettos, leans against a fender
and begs his smack. He whips her once
Ewwwwwww
she mouths and puckers lips to face him,
instead, licks her finger and
puts out the fire on her own hip.

Something in that motion, the finger
sizzling hip alerts Mom and Dad.
The flag, the flag behind her and above
at the bar they've heard about.
And up go the windows, hummed
into containment. The boy mouths something
to Dad who looks forward, worried
wishing he were south of the river
kicking the shit out of someone.

Weena never cares.

There! Another pickup

loaded with men. Faces blue, orange, and white
even more painted than hers. They are wise,
young, and know where they are. Weena on the pageant runway
before them, hands on hips, right stiletto
tapping impatient.

Well? she says.
Show me your tits.

The toe still tapping, men
frozen, watched by all of us
up in the bar. We are more than them
and begin the chant that Weena began, asking
for that one small favour.
And the miracle, the miracle
the Italian or Arab
six-four-no-more-than-22
strips off his jersey
and we are silent, above,
in awe.

Thank you
says Weena, and gently licks his nipple.

The light changes, the turmoil begins
in the pickup as the boy falls back, and Weena is
between lanes waving after them, blowing kisses
that douse fires all over town.

NORM SACUTA is a poet and fiction writer living in Regina, Saskatchewan.
His first poetry collection, *Garments of the Known*, was published by

Nightwood Editions. His fiction has appeared in various magazines and anthologies, and his novel, *One Last Thing About the Titanic,* is nearing completion. His second poetry collection will be coming out in 2012.

Queering the Way
by Voicing Otherness

Holding . . . a poetic monologue (an excerpt)

STEEN (CHRISTINA) STARR

WAITING

It's not that late, really.

We didn't say what time, exactly. Sometime after three, roughly, vaguely, rushed, furtively. It will still ring. Things maybe got in the way. I have lots to do. I could keep doing it, what I have to do. I just need some little detail of a thing to stretch around this silence and make it pop.

I was okay, really, I was okay on my own. I was getting over it.

I don't need the bullshit. Always waiting. Afraid to take the garbage out. Afraid to miss the phone. Always waiting. All my friends, even. They said, "Oh I can't believe how strong you are. How well you're handling it."

Here I am. Ms. Tower of Resistance. Ms. Pick Up the Pieces and No Looking Back.

I am waiting.

I am waiting for the phone to ring so I can say, *Yes, I'm here, come now.* And wait and wait for the kiss, the feel of skin against skin, the rolling in bed and never never wanting to get out, to stop kissing, stop pressing skin on skin, my mouth on skin, on soft moist lips. Oh.

We haven't even done it yet. I mean, we haven't done it since *she* got here. Since we had to stop doing it because *she* arrived with her bags and her desire and her picture of life here totally in love and faithful. All they need is each other. All they need is to be together for perfect happiness and unwavering commitment. Right.

I guess any possibility of that evaporated, like snow in April melting against the heat of the sun, melting the pretty white picture down to hard grey pavement, the first time we kissed.

THE FIRST KISS

We didn't, actually, kiss until much later.

And it was her, of course, who took the prerogative, who leaned across her car in the middle of a k.d. lang song after we'd had dinner and while we were waiting at a light.

I was so pleased and excited and nervous and terrified, having finally asked her out, worrying for two weeks about what to wear and whether to be cool and calm, as if I did this every day, had a date any old night of the week, or tried to be myself, which I don't really know how to do.

And there we were, having dinner. She, unbelievably, across the table from me, her dark eyes warm and attentive, her mouth ready with laughter. All night I swayed from behaving like a smiling, speechless idiot to feeling like Gertrude Stein holding a salon.

And then we were driving back to my place. We'd been talking about ourselves all night and I was still talking, a little drunk—on the wine, on being Gertrude Stein—and suddenly she leaned across the middle of my sentence to kiss me with her open mouth.

I didn't want to stop. I kissed her again and again until the light turned green and the asshole behind us leaned on his horn and we jumped apart and lurched back into traffic and then laughed about it all the way to my house.

We kissed again when she parked the car and then we came inside and kissed and kissed until all our clothes were on the floor and our lips were sucking at much more than our mouths.

She stayed all night and I don't think we slept until the sun reached in to bless my windowsill with light.

LIGHT

And now that light is gone.

That warm precious light
that stroked its way in
where we lay spent and
sleeping in each other's arms.

That light that returned again and again
each time we woke with the sheets on the floor
and taste of sweat on our skin;
that light that arrived with the promise of love like
breakfast served up on a tray.

A light that illuminates nothing.

That reveals only the present minute and
this hand at the end of this arm, her mouth on my fingers,

but nothing of tomorrow,
of the absence that will be illuminated then,
of the transience of sun
across the day.

On a dreary day in 1993 as STEEN (CHRISTINA) STARR was attempting
to recover from her first lesbian-induced broken heart, her talented
actor-sister Rebecca called and asked if she had any ideas for a script.
Holding . . . a poetic monologue was born. It was produced in full at the
Edmonton Fringe Theatre Festival under the direction of Beau Coleman,
where it was nominated for Sterling Awards in Outstanding Production
and Outstanding Visual or Sound Design. Since then, steen has created a
varied trove of theatre and performance works that have been produced
across Canada and in the United States, and her offstage writings are
included in a number of anthologies and online. Check out christinastarr.ca.

The Interview
MARC COLBOURNE

They asked him many questions. Many required the same answer but were asked in different ways. They asked him about the small Nicaraguan community that was his home. He told them, and he remembered the cool wind that came on nights when anything seemed possible. He thought of his small wooden house nestled among the tall trees that offered protection when this same wind became too strong. They asked about the three men who pulled him into a dark alley, forced their way inside him, beat him, and left him bleeding and unconscious. He told them how he remembered their smell and how it had followed him for days. They asked him about Maria: his transgendered cousin who was killed walking home from her best show ever. The police hadn't even bothered to file a report about her death. They wrote it off as one less whore working their streets. But Miguel knew different. Maria would never have sold herself in that way. She was more likely to be found in church on Sunday morning than on a street corner on Saturday night. He told them, and he remembered how her voice rose sweetly over everyone else's when they sang hymns together. They asked him about all of this. And they asked about his family.

↖ ↗ ↘

Miguel was eighteen when he last spoke to his mother. He remembered the moment their relationship went silent. The previous days had been filled with heated arguments marked by uncomfortable silences and dropped sentences. This silence was weighted with the words forbidden to pass their lips. There had been family arguments before. Several of them, in fact. And always they blew over. Not unlike the hurricane winds that battered their small community each November. The heavy winds always left their mark: a fallen roof, destroyed crops, or, in the case of their family disagreements, a bruised cheek or a burning resentment. But always the storms had passed.

Only six months before, Miguel had been happy for perhaps the first time in his life. Truly happy. The reason for this change was Alejandro. Ale lived in a farming community just on the other side of the train station that marked the limits of Miguel's town. To call it a "community" might be a stretch as it was little more than a string of wooden houses connected by a dirt road. At night, the only illumination came from the lights peeking through the places where the thin boards forming the walls of the houses were warped by the November rains.

They had met in the park in the centre of town on a night that could have been like any other. The memory of this encounter still had the power to put a smile on Miguel's face. Both of them were shy but brazened by the homemade rum and their adolescent hormones. Night's end saw them walking together toward the train station. Sitting on the edge of the tracks in the darkness, they had shared what little rum remained in the two-litre coke bottle and laughed, stole glances at each other, talked, and, finally, after what had seemed like a lifetime, kissed. When they finally parted the sun had come up, roosters had made their morning announcements, and the dogs that roamed the streets in packs at night had separated to follow their lone adventures. Miguel had gone to bed that morning feeling different. Older. Wiser. Like he had been granted a glimpse into a secret world. He was in love.

They continued to see each other in secret over the next months. One day, as they were saying goodbye, Ale pressed a crumpled piece of paper into his hand. Miguel could see that it was written on school notepaper, the newsprint variety that was distributed freely to all the students courtesy of a faith-based NGO from some distant country where Miguel was certain that students wrote on paper that didn't tear if you pushed your pencil across it with a little too much force. Miguel had never been outside of his town, much less his country, but he knew this with a certainty that only those who depended on the generosity born of Christian guilt could know.

Miguel read that love letter over and over again until its wonderful words were etched into his memory and he could close his eyes wherever he was and recite the poetry that Ale had gifted him. At night he would sleep with the note safely tucked under the thin pouch stuffed with old T-shirts that was his pillow, and each morning he would slide his hand underneath and find comfort in the touch of the paper.

One morning his hand couldn't find it. Miguel lay there for a moment or two, tried to control his panicked breathing and started tearing the bed apart looking for the cherished words. He wasn't worried about losing the words—they were firmly entrenched in his mind—but he knew that the note's discovery could mean disaster. As he searched, his brother came into his sleeping area and watched him in his madness. His smile could only mean one thing. Miguel's heart sank as he realized that his brother now controlled what would come of the day. Their eyes met but only for a second. His brother turned and left the room.

The next few days were filled with fear and anxiety. But to Miguel's surprise his brother said nothing. Nothing changed. Maybe, thought Miguel, his brother didn't want his life disrupted either. Or maybe he just didn't want to be known as the guy with the maricon for a brother. As time passed, Miguel began to relax.

Almost six months went by without incident. Miguel continued to see Ale. His days were spent restlessly waiting for the protection that the darkness offered them. Each time that they met at the train station, Miguel learned new things about the person who occupied his every thought. But perhaps more important was what he learned about himself. He soon realized that he had the ability to truly love someone and to be open to the vulnerability that only comes from allowing someone to love you in return.

Then he made a fatal mistake. He pissed off his brother during a regular game of dominoes. Nothing serious. Machismo and rum-fuelled fights often broke out over the small wooden blocks. Always they ended with good-natured laughter and a loudly declared promise to win the next game. This time, however, it ended with his brother pulling the yellowed note from his pocket and passing it quietly to his mother as he walked outside for a smoke.

It was three days later that Miguel and his mother stopped speaking. It was suppertime and they were all in the house with the exception of his brother, who had taken an evening job guarding a newly constructed health clinic. Miguel, his sister Marielys, his mother and father were all seated around the old wooden table at the back of the house. Miguel sat, as he always did, with his plate perched on his knee as he didn't trust the table. No one else seemed to notice how it buckled and swayed under the weight of the plates, rice cooker, pot of black beans, and his father's elbows. They each sat in their prescribed places, waited for their mother to start serving the food, and ate noisily. This was their routine. And today was the same as any other day with one major difference. It was quiet. Marielys had just finished telling them that some kid had been found dead on the hill just outside of town.

"They found him this afternoon. Enrique was there . . . he was the one who told me. He must have been there for a couple of days—judging by how swollen he was. Not Enrique . . . the kid.

And he was almost black from the sun, Enrique said. You know who he was? He was that kid that lived by the old church. Just him and his mom. He was fifteen or something. I think he should have been in my year at school, but he stopped coming a couple of years ago. He told me once that he quit because he needed to work after his dad left. But I know he doesn't work. He left because of the things the older boys did to him. They drove him out. You know the boy, Papa . . . the one they used to call la marica, maricon, faggot. What was his name? Miguel, tu sabes?"

Miguel didn't dare to speak. He didn't even look up from his food. He reminded himself to chew the pork and beans that he had just shovelled into his mouth. The hunger that seemed so present just a few minutes ago had disappeared completely. He wanted to be anywhere but here.

"Marco, no? Si. Marco." Marielys answered her own question.

Their father nodded silently in agreement. He also didn't look up from his plate. His father never was a man for conflict or discomfort—unlike his mother—and Miguel was certain that he shared his wish to be as far away from that table and discussion as possible. Finally, Miguel forced himself to look up and stole a glance toward his mother. Her gaze was fixed on him, but her eyes didn't betray any emotion. His plate again captivated his sight, and Marielys, seemingly unaware of the tension, continued her story.

"He had hung himself with the dog's leash. The dog was still there. Imagine that. He wouldn't leave him even after being there for three days. He was growling and snapping at Enrique and the others as they tried to cut him down. They had to kill it to get at him. They had to, Papa," Marielys said as soon as she registered her father's pained expression. He loved animals. Maybe more than people. They didn't require anything difficult from you. "They hit him in the head with a rock. One throw. But that doesn't really matter, I guess." Marielys paused for effect and looked at the faces of her family. Her audience. She wanted to ensure that she held their attention. When she was absolutely certain that her family was engaged, she went on.

"Enrique says he hung himself because el viejo that lives across from the stadium caught him fooling around with some guy that was working on his farm. They say that the old man marched straight to Marco's mother's place and told her what he saw. Can you just imagine?" Marielys always wanted people to *imagine* the scenes in her story. Made it more dramatic and real, she thought. "Anyway, when Marco got home, his mother was crying and told him she didn't want a maricon for a son. His neighbour said that Marco didn't say anything. His neighbour heard everything from her yard. She wasn't trying to eavesdrop—or so she says—but you know how all the gardens are so close together in that part of town. You couldn't help but hear. Even if you tried. Which I am sure she didn't. She is a bit of a gossip, that one." Marielys could sense that she was losing her audience and so she quickly continued. "Anyway, he didn't try to deny it. Or defend himself. *Imagine!*" There it was again. "He just turned around, took the dog as if going for a walk, and left."

There was silence. No one spoke . . . a rare occurrence in their house indeed. Marielys looked from person to person trying to determine if her story had made its desired impact and, seeing that it had, she went eagerly back to her food. She was so busy trying to eat while smiling at her storytelling abilities that she didn't even notice her mother get up from her place at the table.

Miguel's mother, Almeida, was a slight woman. Even people who met her briefly considered to be pretty—beautiful even. Those who knew her on a deeper, or at least more frequent, basis still saw this beauty—but a version of it so tempered by her severity and ability to maim with but a word that they scarcely recognized it as such. Instead she was thought of as solid and deserving of their respect and fear. As she passed him and crossed the floor of the small house without uttering a word, Miguel felt fear.

He saw his mother stoop to retrieve the dog's leash from its place by the front door. She bent slowly, deliberately, as one who is mindful of all of the body's aches and heart's wounds might.

Almeida returned to the table and placed the leash softly—almost tenderly—in front of Miguel. She met his upturned eyes and spoke softly in an unwavering voice,

"Mijo, why don't you do the same?"

She had said it so sweetly that Miguel wasn't sure he had heard correctly. But his sister's rare silence and his father's retreat to the front porch, cigar in hand, confirmed that he had.

It was the last thing his mother ever said to him.

ॱ ॱ ॱ

As he finished his story, Miguel raised his eyes from the flaw in the fake wood grain in the table that had captured his gaze since he had begun to talk. The adjudicator turned her head slightly, busied herself shuffling papers into no real order, and seemed to avoid his eyes. The refugee board lawyer looked at him quietly. Finally the questions ended. He wouldn't have to share anymore. Now the waiting would begin. Eighteen months of it, his counsel had warned him. Eighteen months before someone he had met for an hour and a half would determine if his lifetime of suffering warranted a stamp on a paper. That stamp that would signal their permission to start anew here in Canada—whatever that meant.

Through his writing, MARC COLBOURNE hopes to entertain, inform, and connect readers to important social issues. As a social worker, he has brought an anti-oppressive lens to his work with such marginalized populations as the lesbian, gay, bisexual, transgendered, and immigrant/refugee communities. His love of travel and cultural exploration has inspired him to live and work in Cuba, Bolivia, Costa Rica, and Guatemala. These influences are evident in his written work.

Why Do I Feel Guilty in the Changeroom at Britannia Pool?

SUSAN HOLBROOK

After all, I'm a swimmer, I have a Speedo, I can do a flip turn and a shallow dive, and I can say "breast stroke" without smirking. I even know that spitting in my goggles will reduce the fog, that baby powder in my cap will stop it sticking to itself. It should be clear to anyone who sees my flipping and diving and spitting and powdering that I am legitimate. That three times a week I mingle with a bunch of naked women and it's all on the up and up. I've been doing it for years, starting at six when I routinely showered at the Y with my mother and her swimming buddies.

I lost sleep over those shower scenes back then, due to the parasite problem. In retrospect I can identify tampon strings as my troubling fixation, but at the time I suffered over how to break it to my mother that she and her friends had worms. Athlete's foot wasn't the only thing you could catch at the pool.

You would think that after twenty-five years, I could feign a little nonchalance. But instead I sneak more peeks, get more flustered when I read that sign "inappropriate behaviour will not be tolerated in the changerooms," and forget more quarters in the coin-operated lockers as every season brings me closer to my scatty-brained sexual prime. Sometimes, particularly when I'm low on cash, I scan the lockers to see if other girls have left quarters behind. Nobody else has this problem. These are women who gossip in the showers while soaping up their gleaming thighs, then smile calmly into the wild scream of blow-dryers, wearing nothing but plush coral pink towels wrapped around their waists, chlorine dripping languorously from suits on hooks. Where did they learn to be so blasé, and why don't they ever forget their quarters?

I learned a while back not to go to Adult Swim on weekends. I took "Adult" to mean that I could do some lengths in peace without being blindsided by an inner tube or looking down at my legs later and saying, "Hey, these aren't my Band-Aids." But I found that some guys interpret "Adult" as in "Adult magazines sold here." They lounge in the shallow end. You try to keep your head down as you approach their creepily billowing trunks and the flash of a medallion nestled in chest hair. Beefy arms span the length of the wall and you have to stop short and, in the time it takes you to suck in a breath, one's nabbed you with an irresistible, "Lookin' good" or, "Can you teach me the breast stroke?"

I'm no better. While I usually breathe right, stroke stroke, breathe left, stroke stroke, today I breathe right, stroke, breathe right, stroke, breathe right on the way up the pool, and breathe left, stroke, breathe left, stroke, breathe left all the way back, just so I can keep my foggy goggles fixed on the red suit in the next lane. I'm a creep too.

She's faster than me, she's plump and shiny and slick. She's like the sea lion in the AquaWorld tank, oblivious to me as she undulates past, her nostrils collapsed into slits. I kick as fast as I can, stroke without splashing, imagine I have long, wiry whiskers, trying to catch her notice. I want to be in the sea-lion club. When she stops at the end, I stop too and take off my goggles. I spit in them, eager to prove that I'm très cool. But instead of hitting the mark clean and sharp, the gob remains slung from my mouth, bobbing like a tiny bungee jumper. She looks over and I forget my lips and smile. Then she's off again like a shot, leaving me and my spittle hanging.

I rest my weary AquaWorld tourist muscles in the sauna. I brought the paper so I don't have to concentrate on where to direct my eyes should any naked women come in. I flip to the personals. The straight section is full of older gentlemen seeking slim ladies and affectionate ladies seeking generous gentlemen. I find the usual chasm between genders in the queer section:

Wimmin to Womyn

GF wants to meet someone who likes music,
laughter, animals and quiet walks. If you're
looking for someone to share with, let's
make friends and then, who knows?

Men to Men

My 8" uncut dick needs a hungry hole to
pump into oblivion. Do you have a bubble
butt and shaved balls? Shoot me a message
and let's see who's more oral.

Why don't lesbians have a genital aesthetic? Are we too skittish about objectifying each other? Or could the problem be, as Mr. Rogers explains, that boys are fancy on the outside, while girls are fancy on the inside? Or is it true that men are just hornier? Do I even know what kind of pussy I like? Have I ever met one I didn't like? Is it in fact the lesbians who are so horny we don't have the patience to be discriminating? I press my back against the hot cedar, close my eyes, and compose a proper personal.

My full breasts need some hard sucking
(Okay, they aren't "full," but 8 inches?)

Please.) and my long tongue hungers for a
wet snatch with plenty of meat to grab on
to. Can you give up music, laughter, and
animals for a chance to fist me all night,
taking breathers only to receive explosive
comes under my busy lips and fingers?
Would you rather have a quiet walk along
the sea wall or my thumb jammed into
your lubed-up ass as I . . .

"Hot today, eh?" Sea-lion girl.

"Oh hi. Yeah." I check to make sure my hands still hold the
paper. She isn't wearing her red suit. As she sits across from me
with one leg bent up to her chest and the other swinging off the
bench, I note that her fanciness is not completely on the inside. I
swallow and wonder if inappropriate behaviour would be tolerated
in the sauna.

"You're a Leo, aren't you?" she says knowingly.

"How did you know?" I gasp, amazed. I'm a Capricorn, but
I want to please, and, besides, her confidence is so dazzling I've
begun to doubt my birthday.

"You have a calm about you; you seem comfortable in your
body." Suddenly it's too hot. Why didn't I realize it before, saunas
are unbearably hot. Comfortable in my body? Does that mean I
look like an old quilt or a one-eyed teddy bear? Are my legs crossed
or uncrossed? Do I have worms? I can't remember. I can't breathe. I
could pass out. She's still looking at me. The romance novel phrase
"her eyes are limpid pools" comes to mind, and now I know what
it means. What if I passed out right this minute? I should plan for
it, so I can tumble gracefully to the floor without breaking my nose
or hip. The tiles down there look nice and cool, a great big ice-cube
tray. She's cute. When I come to, I might find her hovering over

me, a concerned look on her face, as she fans me with her flipper. I need to run out, take a cold shower, or move down to the lower bench. At least lose this newspaper, which is about to combust in my lap. But I sit still, comfortable in my body.

"Have you had your Saturn's return?" she asks.

"I don't know. I'm . . . I'm from Calgary."

Is "what's your sign" making a comeback? Did it ever stop working in Vancouver? It's clearly working on me. Why is she so cool? Why don't I put down my paper? I could just put down the paper in a really beyond comfortable way. She's smiling. I'm evaporating. She takes a swig from her Volvic bottle. With a sudden rush of bravado, I toss the paper aside. But with all the heat, it's become affixed to my fingers and I can't shake it. I'm still trying to peel myself off when she gets up to leave. Cool air rushes in as her glossy butt swishes out. The newsprint has made an impression on my silly-putty skin, so now I have "raunchy action" on one thumb and "social drinker" on the other.

I wait a couple of minutes so it doesn't look like I am following. Slink down to the lower bench with arms extended so I can break my fall if indeed I pass out. Finally make it to the shower and wash off the sweat, careful also to scrub my thumbs, since she's probably not into labels.

I approach my locker naked, less because of being comfortable in my body than because I don't want her to see that I stole my towel from the Holiday Inn. Her locker's next to mine. She's about to leave, her boots all laced up, and she's putting on a black rain slicker. I'm buck naked, but I don't care because I'm a Leo. I put my key in and my quarter pings to the floor. While bending over I glance up, look her straight in the limpid pools, which are discovered dilating and travelling over my skin. She turns pink and bolts for the exit. The door to her empty locker swings open, and I pinch the quarter peeking out of her slot.

SUSAN HOLBROOK is author of the Trillium-nominated *Joy Is So Exhausting* (Coach House Press 2009) and *misled* (Red Deer Press 1999), short-listed for the Pat Lowther and Stephan G. Stephansson Awards. She teaches English and Creative Writing at the University of Windsor. She recently co-edited *The Letters of Gertrude Stein and Virgil Thomson: Composition as Conversation*. The "Guilty" series of poems was conceived when she found herself feeling like an interloper in the lingerie department at the Bay.

Sweet Tooth

R.W. GRAY

I

4 ripe avocados, pitted and peeled
6 tablespoons fresh lemon juice
3 cups low-fat plain yogourt
4 large fresh basil leaves, slivered
¼ teaspoon freshly ground pepper
Pinch of salt
4 large fresh basil leaves, for garnish
4 radishes, finely chopped, for garnish

They served a cold soup first, and it seemed like a perfect choice on such a warm evening in early June. The soup had almost been an afterthought, for the rice required so much attention that the soup, and most of the rest of the meal, became insignificant in comparison. Everyone had tasted the rice, a wild breed, and the general consensus was that it was not yet cooked, so more water was added and it was cooked some more, and then more water and more cooking. Wild rice is the most difficult to cook and the grain never reaches the texture one would expect. Eventually, hunger caused the guests to call the rice cooked and brought them to the table, at first without the cold soup.

August's grandmother used to tell her that on particularly hot days one should drink hot tea to cool down. That if one drinks cold liquids the body thinks it is cold and acclimatizes itself accordingly.

So it follows that although the cold soup was refreshing in the heat of an early summer evening, it may have only increased the fervour of those who consumed it. And who would have thought, passion and cold soup.

II

> Two small Italian eggplants, cut into 1-inch cubes
> 1 pound very new potatoes (the kind you can easily hold in the palm of your hand)
> 4 tablespoons olive oil
> 1 green and
> 1 red bell pepper, both cored, seeded, and cut into 1-inch squares
> 1 red onion, coarsely chopped
> 6 ripe plum tomatoes, cubed
> A handful of each of the following: parsley, basil, and oregano
> 2 cloves garlic, minced
> Salt and pepper to taste

They each tell stories of their childhood. Jamie confesses how he made a neighbour boy drink a mix of drink crystals and his own urine. August admits she used to eat things she found on sidewalks, though, as Jamie points out, a hostess should never make such confessions. But it is Robert who tells a story from Tim's childhood. He talks of a young boy without a father. At night his mother must, after a long day on the canning lines, bathe each of his brothers and sisters herself before putting them to sleep. Only after bathing all four children would she draw herself a bath. The boy remembers lying in a tucked-in bed and hearing the sound of rushing water and this sound becomes for him another word for sleep. Even now, as an adult, the sounds of rushing water subdue him and fill him with fatigue. A school trip to Niagara Falls was almost fatal.

Tim blushes, tries to pretend the story hasn't been told, intends to wipe his mouth but can't find his napkin. A polite smile, he looks out the window.

Thinking about water falling, Robert takes Tim's hand under the table. Then he stands and goes to the kitchen to refill the water jug. There, with the jug in his hand and the water beginning to flow cold from the kitchen tap, Robert thinks again of the story he has just told at the kitchen table about Tim as a child. Once, when Tim had a terrible flu, Robert left the water running in their tiny bathroom, wishing he could amplify the sound, longing to ease Tim to sleep. They have been together four times and broken up three, met so many times that they've been able to let go of all the faces that could have kept them apart. But now Tim is moving, to the other coast. And Robert is staying. Irreducible facts.

III

The last bite of food bitten, the cutlery akimbo on empty plates, August gives Jamie a small smile as the heat swells in and replaces the conversation. Outside the windows the cicadas dirge in the swelter, and in the kitchen water rushes through the taps as Robert fills the water jug. Tim stifles a yawn brought on by the sound of rushing water, then blushes.

Jamie wonders if Robert has always been this way, how he fills a room. Robert is the type of man who tells stories while Tim, Jamie notices, is the kind of man stories are told about. Jamie wonders if it's a trick of physiology, suggested by Tim's plump mouth and thick neck. Or maybe because he talks less. Even now, as Tim shyly looks down at his own solid tradesman hands in his lap he leaves much to the imagination. When he brings his glass to his mouth, there is something unconscious and deliberate. A closer look would show how his tongue reaches out to touch the glass, as though he trusts it more than his bottom lip to ensure the rim is there. Robert turns and sees August looking at him too. His mouth, Jamie thinks.

"What were you like as a child?" Tim asks Jamie. August smiles and looks at her husband.

"Smaller, but the same size head," says Jamie.

August and Tim try to think about Robert as a child, how he seems to have come into the world as an adult with no history, no memories, no photos of himself naked at two, sitting in a creek bed. Each of them marvels at how they could love the man without noticing the missing past.

The casserole, too, is a secret recipe, and Jamie hasn't ever given out the ingredients without first forgetting to mention something. Maybe a tablespoon of lemon zest, grated.

IV

And when the meal is mostly finished, August begins to clear the table, walking from the kitchen to the dining room and back again making as many trips as possible in order to avoid either room. In the kitchen, her husband, Jamie, feeds the dog, while in the dining room her past love Robert laughs and tells a story to the one he loves now, Tim. She still can remember the V of his chest hanging over her, the smooth length of his back under her hands. Jamie's back is hairy.

Hands balancing dishes, she glances at Robert, his head tilted down to look at Tim's hands in his.

She passes Jamie, who returns to the table. In the kitchen she wonders if Robert fantasized about a man like Tim when they were together, remembers the small apartment in Winnipeg they shared, the one with too many doors for its two rooms and the late-night scrapes and shouts of ice skaters on the frozen, flooded tennis courts out back. She doubts he remembers.

Stacking dishes next to the sink, she idly tastes a piece of chicken off Jamie's plate. She remembers making the meal, the list of ingredients, she remembers even tasting it to be sure she'd not forgotten anything. She'd put a little too much garlic in the eggplant but not enough salt. But she doesn't remember the taste of the meal as they sat at the table. Someone, maybe Tim, had complimented her and she'd nodded. But she couldn't remember any tastes between the making of the meal and this moment, closing parenthesis over the dirty dishes. An argument for eating alone, without the distraction of other people, she thinks, eating another bite from Jamie's plate.

With a deep breath she returns to the table, poises on the edge of her chair, hoping she might find glasses or side plates that still need to be cleared. Jamie's hand rests on her hip and so she looks at him, reflex. A tender smile. He has a spot of cold soup in the corner of his mouth. She reaches to her feet to find her napkin, expecting it's dropped, but can't find it.

"The corner of your mouth," she says, sticking her tongue out to show him how to reach the spot of soup.

He sticks his tongue out the opposite direction.

"Got it?" he asks.

"Yes," she says and looks away from the spot of soup.

v

It was a dinner punctuated by the hot summer wind rustling the window blinds and the dog running off with the table napkins. Jamie finds her in the kitchen, looking out at the small yard they have behind the house. The first thing they did when they moved into this house was tear up the bricks and plant grass so the dog could play in the 5 x 12 space. A snapshot of a life, but who knew if the dog cared?

Jamie wonders what August is thinking and where she has been with those blue eyes. She cut her index finger while she was slicing the red peppers for dinner, and just the sight of the Band-Aid hurts him. All her family is prone to fainting and she had to sit on the floor with the half pepper in her hand, crushing the waxy texture.

In pain she is unreachable, but this distraction of hers, at least, is familiar to him.

He returns to the table, to their guests, and August returns, perches on her chair surveying the table. She is away and gone. He touches her on the hip with his open palm, cupping her warmth and softly bringing her attention around. He has learned to economize his touch, to express the most affection in the smallest gesture.

How he came so far in this life to this house, this home, this wife with the red pepper seems a mystery to him now. In the other room is his friend, his wife's past lover and the lover's current lover. This dinner's guests.

And this is how it is meant to go. Three years of marriage culminate in a dinner party where the food doesn't satiate the appetite, and the light flush the wine brings masks something stirring. He knows three languages, and yet would he confess in any of them the way he finds himself looking at this young man, Tim, at this dinner party tonight? Perhaps not a kind of thirst, but only an undercurrent on this strange beach. Something he will never let take him away but still . . . there is this strange sensation of colder water pulling on one's feet. Another world, a few feet down.

This young man is the geography of a place he will never visit, only lines on a map he traces lightly with his finger. These subtle loves, these subtle passions are harmless when one is married. The next morning he can blame it on the wine . . . a brash and crass Argentinean grape, incidentally, though the guests liked it.

The kettle calls from the kitchen and his wife walks from the room with a consoling smile. Even a stranger could see she is a dancer. A ballet dancer, since it must be known that dancers from different forms walk differently. Modern dancers pound the earth with their feet, expecting some answer in return. But this woman, a ballet dancer, seems always, always about to rise up through the ceiling on an unexpected current, limbs like jellyfish tendrils, to disappear suddenly one Sunday afternoon so quietly even the dog would not start barking.

And then what? What would this man, her husband, do then? He can't float away. Not in this body at least, corduroy and belly flesh. It's a body that has worn him well, but some days, lately, it feels like laundry day underwear, the saddest most shameful pair. He's still in very good shape, but after each run the small of his back clenches and whines. More often than not, he wants to stay home on weekends with the dog and the comfort of knowing August will be there soon with something chocolate she's found at the local patisserie. She loves him in a Hansel and Gretel way.

Growing older with half-imagined passions and a sweet tooth. The crème brûlée. The forgotten dessert. He moves to the fridge, removes the small ceramic dishes full of cream (he jokingly calls them pudding for adults), and follows his wife into the dining room. For the briefest moment as the kitchen door swings open he catches sight of Tim and Robert holding hands across the corner of the table, before they turn to greet him or the dessert.

VI

Robert watches first August, then Jamie enter the room from the kitchen. He remembers reading somewhere that if both of your hosts are in the kitchen for more than three minutes, all is not well, and despite the small dimple that has formed between August's eyebrows, there is no evidence of a disagreement on Jamie's face.

In the middle of a joke, and to punctuate his description of the jarring his sister's car caused the house when she drove into it, Robert bumps the hanging lamp above the dining room table with his palm. For the rest of the evening the light will continue to sway, as though on a ship in open waters.

Laughter ricochets between the wineglasses, followed by a silence in which they each think of sleep and wonder if the evening has not gone on too long. Tim takes Robert's hand underneath the table, and August wipes adult pudding from the corner of Jamie's mouth with her bare hand.

VII

4 separated egg yolks
2 cups of fresh cream
½ cup sugar
1 tablespoon real vanilla
1 cup brown sugar

The taste of the crème brûlée is indescribable. One man would call it "better than sex," another would say "a pleasure unlike any other," and yet another would only smile and say that "time is measured more carefully, more painfully with a good dessert." And you see, the woman said nothing. For it was painful enough for her to hear the men diminish such pleasure. With each spoonful she languished, tasted each mouthful as though alone in the room.

The final scraping of the small, white, porcelain bowls signals an end to this dinner. Two men will leave and one will stay. The woman and the man will leave the dishes soaking in the sink and will fall asleep, each to their own side of the bed.

The dog sleeps in the kitchen tonight, dreaming to the taunting smell of dinner's dishes piled high in the sink.

R.W. GRAY was born and raised on the northwest coast of British Columbia and received a PhD in Poetry and Psychoanalysis from the University of Alberta in 2003. His first book of short fiction, *Crisp*, was published by NeWest Press in 2010. He is also the author of two serialized novels in *Xtra West* magazine and has published poetry in various journals and anthologies, including *Arc*, *Grain*, *Event*, and *dANDelion*. He has also had ten short screenplays produced, including *Alice & Huck* and *Blink*. He currently teaches film at the University of New Brunswick in Fredericton.

tassels
BEREND MCKENZIE

There is a knock at my bedroom door. I manage to hide the skipping rope behind my back as my dad opens it.

"Dad! I thought we said that when I turn seven, you would start knocking."

I don't remember that agreement.

"I need my privacy, Dad!"

Buddy, you and I made plans to watch Roots *on* TV *tonight. 8:00. You, me,* Roots, *and a big bowl of popcorn. Don't forget.*

"Great. I can't wait!"

↖ ↗ ↘

I'm actually seven-*and-a-half* years old and my sister just gave me her bright pink skipping rope.

I'm moving on, she said.

It has multicoloured metallic tassels on each handle. I love these tassels. I love the rubbery smell it leaves on my hands after I skip. I love how I can stretch it out till the bright pink of the rubber turns to white and back to pink when I release it. I love the way I can see the shiny tassels twinkling as I skip. I love my skipping rope!

Sometimes I take it down into the basement when no one else is around and practise. It becomes something that is mine and mine alone. It takes my mind off my problems and is an excuse for me to run away and be by myself.

It sits and waits, tucked away in a secret pocket in my school knapsack. At the drop of a hula hoop, any moment—as long as no one's watching—I take out my pink, brightly tasselled rope and skip till I need a puff on my inhaler. I can get up to 150 now.

Darlene Boyle is toast.

↖ ↗ ↘

Ever since I was a baby my father has carried me around on his shoulders.

When you are up there I feel like a king, he says.

I hold on to his forehead with my small hands to steady myself as he lifts me up and carries me to the living room for the beginning of *Roots.*

Do you remember what this show is about?

"Black people?"

And?

"Africa?"

What else?

"Slavery, Daddy?"

That's right. A long time ago, people like you were brought to America and forced to work for free.

"How come?"

Because they had darker skin.

"So if I was living back then I would be a slave?"

Yes. Buddy, there are people who may not like you because you are different.

"No way!"

Off you get. Do you want something to drink?

"Umm, some Kool-Aid, please."

I watch the introduction of *Roots* with deepening curiosity. I am excited to see a TV show filled with black people. Dad returns with the bowl of popcorn and my drink. We sit and watch all the episodes together.

At first I feel uncomfortable watching the black people living in Africa. Everyone walks around almost naked. Boy, . . . am I glad to be Canadian. Everyone has to wear shirts to school here.

I am surprised to see people of colour kissing and carrying on normal relationships like my white parents.

"Did you and Mommy buy me, Dad?"

No, we adopted you.

"Did you change my name the way Kunta Kinte became Toby?"

No. Your name has always been Buddy.

"Did you want a Negro boy?"

We wanted another little boy. We didn't care what colour you were. As long as we got to love you.

It's late, way past my bedtime, and Dad is tucking me in.

"Am I a nigger, Daddy?"

No! You're not! And if anyone ever says anything like that to you I want you to let me know. Promise?

"I promise."

Now get some sleep. Love you.

"Love you more."

↖ ↗ ↘

I know every element of grade four skipping; Chinese Skipping, Double Dutch, and Spanish Dancers. I can go salt *and* pepper. I can go backwards, forwards—and even crisscross. Oh—I am good.

At school I watch the girls skip at recess, to check out my competition. Envy seeps out of every pore because I can't join them. Because even I know that boys don't play with girls. Me skipping with girls at recess would mean me getting beat up after school. I'm not going to give Nelson Weaver another chance. He already thinks I'm a freak.

Darlene Boyle is the best. She's a tall farm girl who always has food stuck in her braces. But I know I'm better than her.

I always ignore the urge to skip with my girlfriends, until today. Today my best friend Christine asks me to come and join them. I don't even think twice. I leap to my feet. I practically fly into the middle of the long spinning rope.

> Spanish Dancers do a kick, kick, kick!
> Spanish Dancers do the splits, splits, splits!
> Spanish Dancers turn a round, round, round!
> Spanish Dancers get out of town!

I did it! My first time! It was a perfect entrance, a stunning exit, and I knew every move! Christine says I am as good as Darlene. Then she says . . . *There should be a skip-off!* Before I can say no, she grabs Darlene, who says, *We'll see about that. What are you going to skip with? That booger hanging out of your nose?*

"No, as a matter of fact, Darlene, I have my own rope."

Well go get it then. Let's see your skipping.

There's no way out. Not with all the girls watching. And I *know* I can beat her! I reach into the secret pocket in my school knapsack and pull out my pink, tasselled rope.

Pepper . . . Backwards . . . On one foot! Ready?

"Oh, I am so ready."

Oh, you are so going down.

One . . . two . . . three . . . four . . . five . . . I'm doing it!

Nine . . . ten . . . eleven . . . twelve . . . this is a piece of cake!

Sixteen . . . seventeen . . . eighteen . . . nineteen . . . twenty . . . twenty-one . . . twenty-two . . . twenty-three . . . twenty-four . . . twenty-five . . . she's getting tired—

Thirty . . . thirty-one, thirty-two, thirty-three . . . her foot catches on her rope but she keeps going—

Forty . . . forty-one . . . forty-two . . . God I love these tassels!

Fifty . . . fifty-one . . . fifty-two . . . Oh my God, Darlene Boyle's going down! I'm still going strong! I'm gonna win! I'm gonna win!

The girls are all cheering me on!

Then I see Nelson Weaver heading toward us.

Look, guys, Toby's skipping like a fag!

My foot gets caught in the skipping rope.

"My name isn't Toby."

Yes it is. It's your slave name.

All the girls go quiet.

Oh yeah, you're right. Your real name is Kunta Kinte!

I can feel every stare. I just lay at Nelson's feet. Frozen. My skipping rope twisted around my legs. I can't move. Nelson bends down and yanks at the skipping rope.

Good to see you brought this with you today. Come on, guys, you hold him down while I teach this nigger a lesson.

The girls move away and the group of boys advances.

He flicks my rope in the air.

What's your name, slave?

"You know what my name is, Nelson."

No, I want you to say it! I want you to say, 'My name is Toby'! Say it or I'll whip you like a slave!

He flicks my skipping rope and it nicks my cheek—but I grab it—and I don't let go.

Nelson pulls—and I don't let go.

He jerks it hard—and I don't let go.

He starts to walk backwards pulling me along the ground—and I don't let go.

The skipping rope starts to stretch until the bright pink of the rubber turns to white—and I don't let go.

The recess bell rings.

I let go. And run.

↖ ↗ ↘

I sit at my desk with my head in my arms so no one can see me cry.

I feel a tap on my shoulder. It's Darlene. She hands me my rope. Most of the tassels have been torn off and it's covered in dirt, making the bright pink rubber look dull and lifeless.

You're going to need this to skip with us tomorrow.

"Thanks, Darlene."

Nelson's in the desk behind me. *Yeah, I'm gonna need it when I whip your ass. After school.*

Five minutes before the bell rings, I tell the teacher that I'm meeting my mother out front for a doctor's appointment. Even though I don't have a note, she lets me go. I run down the hall and out of the school. I pass a garbage can and I toss the skipping rope in.

I look back one last time. What's left of the sparkly tassels catches the sunlight. It moves in the breeze. It looks like it's waving to me. I wave back.

↖ ↗ ↘

I sit on the edge of my bed and chew on my nails. They are bleeding but I don't stop. I hear my dad's car pull into the garage. I hear him enter the house. I hear his heavy footsteps on the stairs. He knocks on my door.

"Come in."

Hey, Buddy. How was school today?

I can't lift my head to look at him. If I do, I know I will start crying.

Your mom said that you barely said hello when you came home. You didn't even ask for a chocolate chip cookie. That's not like you.

My lip starts to quiver, but I still don't say anything. Dad comes and sits on the bed beside me and pulls me onto his lap.

He moves my chin up with his finger until our eyes meet. I can't control myself any longer and bury my face in his chest. Between giant sobs, I tell him everything.

↖ ↗ ↘

At dinnertime I am quiet. I can't eat. When it's over, I get up to start the dishes.

Your sisters will do your chores for you tonight. Go down and get your coat.

I do so without saying a word.

The car ride is silent except for the sound of the engine and my dad's grinding teeth. He only grinds his teeth when he is mad.

He stops the car in front of a rundown house. All the lights are on and I can see everyone inside is sitting down eating dinner.

Keep your head up the whole time. Don't look at your shoes. Don't look around you. Don't be afraid. Do you remember what we talked about?

"Yes."

We get out of the car. I walk up the sidewalk behind him, dragging my feet. I feel sick to my stomach.

Dad waits with me at the front door.

He puts his arm on my shoulder.

Ring the bell, Buddy.

A big tall man opens the door and asks what we want.

Is Nelson here?

The big man tells us Nelson is in the middle of dinner.

This will only take a second, my dad says, pulling me in front of him so that I am now standing just inside the doorway.

The man calls out. We wait. It feels like forever.

Nelson comes up behind Mr. Weaver.

I just keep staring forward. Like my dad told me.

Nelson's mouth falls open when he sees me.

I clench my fists but look him straight in the eye.

My legs are wobbly but I look him straight in the eye.

I pull away until I don't feel my father's hand on my shoulder anymore and look him straight in the eye.

"Nelson, don't ever call me a nigger. Ever again."

Nelson looks at his father, then back at me. There is a long silence, father staring at father, son staring at son.

Okay.

Mr. Weaver asks my dad how he knew where Nelson lived.

I'm a cop. It's a small town. Have a good night.

After the door closes, my dad bends down and lifts me onto his shoulder. I hold on to his forehead with my small hands to steady myself.

I'm so proud of you. I think you deserve a treat after that. Tomorrow I'll take you to a toy store. What are you going to get?

"A skipping rope, Daddy."

Oh yeah, what colour?

"I think . . . a blue one this time. Bigger tassels."

BEREND MCKENZIE is an award-winning writer, actor, playwright, and producer. He has had multiple pieces performed at Edmonton's L&Q Cabaret, including *The Munts shorts* and *Blood Bath at St. Paul's.* His first play was the outrageous Queer puppet show for adults, *Get Off the Cross, Mary!*

"tassels" is from Berend's Jessie Award-nominated second play, *nggrfg*, which has been performed across Canada. *nggrfg* premiered in Toronto at The Susan Douglas Rubes: Young People's Theatre in 2011. Berend won the Best Actress Award at the 2001 Vancouver International Fringe Festival for his portrayal of Charlotte in Christopher Durang's *Beyond Therapy.* As an actor, he has worked with Academy Award-winning actresses Halle Berry and Angelina Jolie.

Queering the Way

by Creating New Artistic
Landscapes

The Unrestrained Homosexual
PETER FIELD

"Are we to become a hedonistic nation of unrestrained
homosexuality, abortion, immorality and lawlessness?"
—Jerry Falwell

SCENE ONE: THE UNRESTRAINED HOMOSEXUAL AT THE
GROCERY STORE.

Sound of Safeway cash register hubbub.

Cashier: Hi, how are you?

Homo: Fine, thanks, you?

Cashier: Great. Air Miles?

Homo: Nope.

More cash register beeping.

Cashier: Will that be everything for you, sir?

Homo: Yup.

Cashier: That'll be $35.20 please.

Takes money.

Thank you.

Returns change.

And that's $4.80 in change. Thanks. Have a great day.

Homo: You too. Bye.

Blackout.

SCENE TWO: THE UNRESTRAINED HOMOSEXUAL AT THE GAS STATION.

The homo drives in. Ding ding!

Gas Jockey: Hi. Fill 'er up?

Homo: Yeah, regular please.

Gas Jockey: Check the oil?

Homo: No, it's fine.

Sound of car being filled with gas.

Gas Jockey: Thirty-four dollars please.

Homo: Here you go.

Gas Jockey: Thanks, have a great day.

Homo: You too. Bye.

Blackout.

SCENE THREE: THE UNRESTRAINED HOMOSEXUAL AT FAMILY DINNER.

Mom enters with plates. They sit on the couch.

Homo: What channel should we watch?

Mom: Let's see what's on the news.

Homo: Okay.

He switches channels and they watch.

Blackout.

SCENE FOUR: THE UNRESTRAINED HOMOSEXUAL HAVING SEX.

In the dark.

Homo: Uh uh uh uh uh uh ugh ugh UH! Oh God, ugh ugh
          UH UNH UNH. OHHHH.

Pause, heavy breathing.

          God.

Long pause. Did you come?

Homo arrives just as the ticket is started.

Homo: Hey! I was just leaving!

Meter Guy: Uh, I already started writing it up—you know how
it is.

Homo: Fuck!

Blackout.

PETER FIELD has worked as a painter, sculptor, set designer, and festival designer. Other than "The Unrestrained Homosexual," he only writes, badly, when he has a broken heart. He can be reached at peterfield.ca.

The Flood
KRISTY HARCOURT

Ten years ago, I posed for a portrait and it changed my life. I was twenty-two years old, only out for a couple of years, barely attending my last year of university. The Edmonton that I knew had a chip on its shoulder, obsessed by all that we weren't. Alberta was "redneck and proud!" Our homophobic reputation was a lazy punchline we'd all heard and lived. Our community connected over common obstacles—a hostile government and, for many, the closeted insecurity that stems from life where being out could risk your job. Those were the years between Delwin Vriend's firing for being gay and the Supreme Court decision that would protect our human rights.

Then, as now, it was always a bit surprising when people came to Edmonton from away—queer people especially—but here he was, Spencer, a gay painter from Ontario. He wanted to collect stories about being gay and about bashing, for an art show. Most people received him with a mixture of suspicion and curiosity. We assumed he came to air our dark secrets, never considering we might have beauty worth reflecting.

He would interview people and paint through the fall, showing the final work, called *The Fag Project*, at Latitude 53 Gallery in January. Daring myself, I signed up as a subject and went to meet him in a grungy studio above the gallery, in one of the dark former warehouses on 104th Street. I posed for a portrait and answered questions about being a dyke in Alberta, my fears, friends, family.

We talked after and I liked him, offered to help spread the word about his project, and we became friends.

He was an "artist in residence," a creative sponsorship that got him a room to stay in and a studio to paint in, in the former nurses' residence behind the Misericordia Hospital. The ominous themes of the work blended perfectly with the spooky location. The building seemed alive with unexplainable sounds and lights; phantom elevators that would chime and open with no one there. I spent most of those months in that odd empty building, hanging out, skipping class, listening to music, and watching layers of paint come to life.

The works varied—the smallest were portraits of people who had offered stories, painted on the fronts of old hardcover books chosen for their loaded titles. Mine was *Not Like Other Girls*. The books were mounted on canvases with quotes from our interviews behind them.

After posing, I hadn't given the portrait much thought. I was caught up in the excitement of helping to build and publicize a major art show. January came and the show opened at Latitude. When I saw my portrait, hanging next to a window in the gallery, I felt sick. Anxious. Exposed. In it, I was wearing a necklace my brother had made me. That's when I stopped wearing it. I heard later that one of the other subjects bought his portrait. He said it was to support the show financially, but I'm not so sure.

Working on *The Fag Project* had a huge impact on my life and career, but until the flood, I somehow tricked myself into forgetting that I had also been one of its subjects, that I had been in it.

The central work was made of two long canvases, each seven feet tall and thirty feet long, hung as an oval room you could walk into and around. On the outside was text, a letter home to his parents about the work and about falling in love with Edmonton. On the inside, the walls were black and bursting forth with fragmented images—the bashers as described from people's stories—men seen, felt, feared, and imagined.

Viewers would walk into the middle and see fears from the inside. Surrounded. Shadowy partial men—only a torso or a fist, a face in profile, a leer, a switchblade, a baseball bat. A muscular arm idly dangling a beer bottle by the neck. A hand resting a thumb on the buckle of a belt. The fragments were like memories, flashes of this detail or that. Like after violence when you tell your story and while you have details, they aren't useful. Recalling a rodeo belt or a company cap, a gleeful, manic laugh.

When you stood inside the canvas room, the walls moving slightly with the motion of other viewers, hearing the sounds of their feet and voices, strange things happened.

People would startle, swear they saw the figures move. The bottle swiftly turn to strike. The hand undoing the belt.

Baseball bats were such a common element of people's stories and fears that they got their own display in the gallery: stacked and carefully wrapped with bows made of bandages.

↖ ↗ ↘

Since that time, Spencer and I have been long-distance friends. We've shared dinner when life has brought us to the same city, called when the other held the key to solving some puzzle. I've built a career teaching about vulnerability and survival, built a life and a home in Edmonton. He's pursued a master's degree based on the project, and I've teased him over the years, lovingly suggesting that the time may have come to let someone else delve into our horrors and to turn his sights to something less goddamned depressing.

This past July, I thought of him when flood rains fell in the same week, here and in Peterborough, Ontario, where Spencer lives. I called him, looking to trade stories, and got his machine.

His voice was slow and disbelieving: *"Hi, it's Spencer. Thanks for your call. Yes, it's true. My studio was completely submerged in the flood. Everything was destroyed."*

Six weeks later, in September, he called back. Said he was crawling out from under the shock and confirmed the worst. He said, *"Everything was destroyed. Over two hundred paintings, papers, photos. Everything. I'm sorry I haven't called you. I couldn't. I have this nightmare, I'm throwing you out. I had to throw you in the garbage. Your portrait. There was sewage in the water so it all became an E. coli risk and in the dream I'm throwing you out, over and over."*

It's okay, I told him. *I'm okay. I'm still here.*

The flood had come in the middle of the night—a summer's worth of rain falling in hours. His studio was below street level next to a gallery. Water and sewage filled to the roof in twenty minutes—so swiftly that a heavy table rose with such force it broke through the ceiling. He learned of it in his car when the CBC listed damaged sites, including the local radio station that was his upstairs neighbour.

He tells me of desperately trying to salvage paintings caked thick with muck. He took them to his parents house to hose them off, finally resorting to the chlorine in their little backyard pool. A friend who came to help found him swimming with a canvas and feared he'd gone insane.

The work that had such an influence on me now lives only in my dreams, night after night, watery dreams of baseball bats, swinging ghostly. When the flood struck, there were two hundred bats stored in the studio. They floated when the water surged in, spinning, beating the paintings and canvases. I picture the bats come to life, swinging in the rushing water, shredding every image of the survivor subjects who conjured them.

KRISTY HARCOURT is proud to be a long-time contributor and co-host of the Loud & Queer Cabaret and to have been connected with this unique gathering of artists and community members to tell our stories. She enjoys capturing snippets of Edmonton's and Alberta's Queer history (real and imagined) for the stage—including *The True Lesbian History of the Calgary Stampede* and *The Flood*. L&Q has given her unique experiences such as the cleavage-toss, crank-calling hate mongers, and her annual duty as adult pleasure product colour commentator. She thanks all of the L&Q family for years of fun, including: Darrin, Kevin, Ron, Neon, Michael, Lulu, and the wonderful actors, writers, musicians, and audiences who've joined us. Special thanks to Spencer Harrison and Trevor Anderson: inspiring artists and friends.

Kristy has been active in Edmonton's Queer communities for nearly two decades, receiving the 1998 Maureen Irwin Exceptional Lesbian Award. For twelve years, she was a host of *Gaywire* on CJSR Radio. Kristy lives in Edmonton with her partner, Christine, their daughter, Jenny, and faithful terrier, Lucy, surrounded by a wonderful network of friends and extended family. By profession, Kristy is an educator who teaches about creating safer communities free from violence.

Birthday
TREVOR SCHMIDT

"Just don't start taking it up the ass, Junior," she says, and she points at me with the cherry of her cigarette. She's loud enough that the few other diners look up from their eggs with their mouths open.

"When you start takin' it up the ass, well, that's when it's all over. 'Cause that's when they know they've got you. You know." Her lips are dark purple, and the stain creeps up the lines around her mouth and makes it look like a big, dark, purple, wet spider that chews and talks and blows smoke at me.

"That's when things started getting real bad between your dad and me. It all turned to shit when I let him start up the ass."

Sylvia, I say, and I look away from the dish-faces that stare at her, slack-jawed.

She notices, and glares at them, her mouth twisting, and they quickly return to their plates. I wrap my hands around my mug and look into my coffee. It's cold.

"You can be gay if you want, that's your choice, Junior, there's nothin' wrong with that, but you're no fag." And she takes a long drag, the smoke drifting half her face away.

Then she's quiet for a while, and I close my eyes and wish it could last forever. It won't, of course, and soon she is chewing loudly, smacking and slurping, and I wonder how a plate of food can take so long.

"So . . ." and there's a long pause and I know she must be

looking at me, squinting under the droop of her eyelashes glued on too low. "*So . . . how's your . . . friend?*"

He's fine, I say quickly, and I sound bored and brutal, and she ought to know that the conversation's over. She ought to, but she doesn't and she stumbles into her next jerky, uncertain sentence. She's uncomfortable, and I don't want to make it any easier. For once, the words don't pour from her like drool.

"*So . . . you're . . . happy? . . . with your friend?*"

(sigh) Yup.

"*Oh . . . Good. Good. I . . . I want you to be happy, Junior.*"

Her hand snakes across the table toward mine, white and scaly. I pull mine away, fast. I've been burned by her before.

She crumples then, ages, and sinks in on herself. She looks so much . . . older than I remember, older than last time. Softer, and rounder, like a dusty pillow with the stuffing coming out.

Oh, great. She's getting all cracked and wobbly. She's going to cry again, like last time. She stubs her cigarette out on the runny yellow-orange centre of her egg, clear through the whole wheat toast beneath it. It sizzles, and we both stare at it, until it fizzles away and smoulders.

Her voice, when it comes again, is a little-girl voice, lost, high, and tremulous.

"*Heard from Robbie?*"

No.

No. I haven't heard from Robbie.

He's gone, Sylvia . . . Robbie is gone. You know that. Better than anyone.

"*I only thought—He's your brother.*"

Robbie's gone. Years ago. You know that.

And we're not going to hear from him. Ever.

"*Do you . . . do you think he's out there?*"

No.

No.

"He has dark, curly hair."

Sylvia. Mom. Robbie's gone. You know that. You remember.

"I meant . . . your friend. He . . . he has dark hair."

Relief. Yes. Yes, that's right, Sylvia. He does. You remember. Good. You remember.

Sylvia nods like a scolded child, silent, and her nose drips, running into her purple spider-mouth.

Robbie had black, curly hair, not like mine at all. I asked her once where my hair came from and she said she wasn't sure . . . didn't know.

I didn't look like my father, or Robbie. Or even my sister, Marie.

No, I was the last one born, the youngest, with this hair, and I soon knew I didn't belong. I was always different.

My father was very tall, and very thin, and very quiet, and when he spoke, it was always in vague parables and metaphors. The thought of him and Sylvia—all round and pink and faded blond and so direct—well, they just didn't go together. The thought of him and Sylvia, and this new revelation that he treated her like a boy in bed—who likes to think of it?

Oh God, she's snivelling again and people are looking. Not that I care, really. Not that I'll ever come back here again until next year. They're not people who matter to me.

I should be at home in bed beneath the warm maroon down comforter. I shouldn't even be out of bed this early on a Sunday, but . . .

We meet every year on April 17. Robbie's birthday. My mom and me meet every year. Marie used to do it too, the three of us, but then it was the job, or the kids, or what-have-you. Nowadays she doesn't even make up an excuse.

Come to think of it, I haven't heard from Marie in a long time.

My dad never came, on Robbie's birthday.

We never miss it, Sylvia and me.

Usually, it's raining, like it is today.

"Junior . . . you still sing?"

No. Well, technically yes. It's still my job. Five nights a week, three sets a night, nine, ten-thirty, and midnight. Long nights in a piano bar, my hands on the black and white keys, the same playlist over and over, the same requests for "Feelings" and "My Way," trying to tune out the clink of glasses and cutlery. The endless nights of drunks and barflies, lonely people, scanning the crowd for a face I might recognize. Or more likely, just closing my eyes and singing like there's no tomorrow.

If she means do I sing like I used to, because I enjoy it . . . ?

No. I don't sing anymore. Much.

"You had such a sweet voice. Shame."

Sylvia looks like shit. I suppose I look okay. I take pains to do my hair and I don't go out without getting myself together. But if she looked at me—if she looked closely—she'd see that I'm not in a good way. Not really. But she won't. Notice, I mean. She's too wrapped up with her own . . . stuff.

Quit crying. I push the napkin at her and I sound mean when the words are out. She takes it and wipes her nose, even though there's a coffee ring dried on it.

"I keep thinkin' . . . I keep thinkin' maybe we'll hear from him," she sniffles, and I turn to look out the window, the rain on the panes, blue, my own white face reflected back, like a skull.

It's been raining for days now. Dad used to say when it rains it means God is crying.

Well—if it's true, God's been pretty miserable lately.

I hate Sylvia for a minute, fiercely and viciously hate her. Her eyes, ringed in blue, blink over her coffee cup. She looks dumb and I hate her.

Then it's passed, and she's my mother again, a pale frayed,

faded version of the old-days Sylvia from when I was little. She was pretty without makeup, and slim, and she had nails then, painted, not chewed away with half-moons of dirt under the edges.

She was my mom and she was almost perfect.

(*Hums.*)

"The Girl from Ipanema" comes through the speakers, and our eyes meet. We're both humming. Her eyes crinkle into a smile and I can't help it. I smile back.

I don't want her to think I like being here with her. Next thing you know she'll be calling me at home in the middle of the night and I'll have to pay to have the number changed again. I ought to think of something serious.

I don't like that she's drawn a comparison between my "friend" and Robbie—that they have the same hair. I thought of it, once, myself. I don't like the thought behind that comparison. The insinuation. I really don't.

"Junior. Junior. Tell it again. Tell me what happened, like I don't know. I think about it all the time, you know, and I been forgetting it all a little. Tell me again. Just so I don't lose it. I don't want to lose anymore."

When I finish the story, when I tell her the whole truth again, it will be over and I can go home for another year. It's time for the story, for both of us, so I close my eyes, take a deep breath, and begin—

Stories like this should take place at night, in the dark, cold, dark nights on the highways, slick, and lightning cracking the sky into pieces.

Her eyes blink, eager and sharp like an owl. *"But it wasn't like that, was it, Junior?"* and she's shaking her head already because she knows the answer.

No, Sylvia. It wasn't like that.

"Nonononononononononono . . ."

Shh.

There is a family in a car on a hot, hot August day, on a straight ribbon of highway, passing through fields of rapeseed in the middle of the prairies.

"Rape's yellow, heh?"

Yes.

It's a hot day—

"Hot hot hot."

◄ ◄ ◄

—and inside the station wagon—cream with wood panelling—the family is restless. The windows are all rolled down, letting in warm air. The red-haired boy sits on the hump, like always, between the sullen teenaged girl with the spotty chin and braces and the boy with dark, curly hair who hangs his fingers out the window, cool. The mother with yellow hair and the yellow terrycloth one-piece fans herself in the front seat and sighs. The dad drives.

They hate each other on this trip, all of them. They have slept too close in the camper trailer that they drag behind them. They haven't bathed today, they are sweating the smell of campfire, and they just want to get home through this flat stretch of road, so flat and bare that there aren't even any trees to break things up and make it interesting.

Oh, and the radio is broken.

The hump is an awful place to be. You're too far from the window, there's nowhere to put your arms. No one talks to you except to say mean things. You can't sing, even quietly, and when the dark-haired boy throws your crossword game book out the window the mother's arm swings into the backseat wildly and the dad swerves the car onto the gravel shoulder and the car slams to a stop, the dust passing over you all.

The mother screeches and swings and you want to cry but you

don't, no, and the boy says that word, that bad word, and he's out the door as the mother lunges over the seat, landing in your lap, her heels kicking the girl in the braces, blood.

The whole family ends up on the side of the road, no one in sight from as far as you can see in one direction to the other.

The girl bloodied and crying, her spotty chin spattered.

The boy cursing and spitting, his T-shirt torn in his escape from the car, his back to the yellow field.

The mother's face is red, purple, the veins standing out in her neck and forehead. One of her breasts has jumped free of its terrycloth casing. It stares at the boy like a third angry red eye.

The dad just watches.

The mother flails at the dark-haired boy, raining blows down upon his head and arms, nails through the air like red knives. She pummels him down like a hammer, sinking him to his knees, then the ground, where he turns on his side like a baby and lies still, whimpering like a bad puppy.

The mother turns back and both her breasts are bare now, the eye-nipples pointing in opposite directions, making the red-haired hump-boy think of the Cookie Monster.

The dad says, "Well, a change is as good as a rest." The mother pulls her top up, blind, and the girl bends over and throws up on the gravel. The boy moans and the mother pronounces:

"You can *walk* for a mile, Mr. Smarty-Mouth, think you're so much brainier than everyone else, that'll teach ya. You can *walk* for a mile and then see who's in charge."

And the family piles back into the car. It smells of sweat and heat and, faintly, of puke. The red-haired boy sits on the hump. Habit.

The dark-haired boy slides by the open window as the car moves away. He looks right at the red-haired boy. Right at him.

↖ ↗ ↘

Her hand on my sleeve brings me back.

"What happened then?"

We waited. We're big waiters, our family is, Sylvia. We waited over the little hill for Robbie to catch up. We sat with the doors open, our legs out, sharing a warm Mountain Dew.

"Just to teach him a lesson. That's all."

Yeah. We're big teachers, too.

And when we went back—

"He was gone."

No trace. No prints. No cars. Nothing.

"Nothing."

↖ ↗ ↘

The mother squats at the side of the road, crying, her hands dragging through the gravel, wiping away the non-footprints that don't exist. The girl stands, numb, her lips swollen, her eyes red and unblinking. The dad stands at the edge of the rape, calling out the boy's name.

"Robbie . . . Robbie . . . Robbie . . . Well, that's cutting off your nose to spite your face. Mother?"

But the mother lies down and cries, racked with sobs, gravel sticking to her legs and face, her mascara smeared like tar. They wait till dark, when he should be scared and cold. They wait for him to come out of the rapefield, sheepish for making them angry or laughing at how he worried them. They wait. But he never comes. Not when the sun is gone. Not when they hear the wild dogs howling. Not when they open the camper and settle in. Not when the lights go out. Not when they pack up in the morning and leave.

He never comes.

↖ ↗ ↘

"He never comes . . . "

The waitress brings a muffin—bran and berry—with a candle in it.

"Someone's birthday?" she inquires.

Yeah. Someone's, I mumble and she leaves it between us.

She picks the candle out carefully and wraps it in a napkin before putting it, oh-so carefully, in her beat-up old purse next to the wadded-up Kleenex and half-empty pill bottles. It's almost refreshing to see that her doctors still think medication could help her. My father's voice rings distant in my head: "An apple a day keeps the doctor away." Well, plant a tree, Sylvia, that's what I think.

When we step out into the parking lot, the sky has broken a bit, the clouds are moving off. There's still no sun. It's grey.

I don't offer to drive her anywhere, although I could, I have a car. I let her kiss me, with her purple lips and smelling of coffee and cigarettes and sorrow. I make a mental note to wipe it off later. I don't tell her that I am going home to an empty house. That my bed is empty too. That my "friend" left a long time ago. Said that I had issues to work out. Emotional distance, and commitment issues.

Family stuff.

I'm not going to wait. I'm not much of a waiter, anymore, anyway.

Anyway.

↖ ↗ ↘

I don't tell her that when we drove away, when Robbie looked right at me . . . he winked.

I don't know what he meant. Did it mean, *Watch this. I'll show them?* Or did it mean . . . If it's some kind of trick, some game, it's gone a bit far. More than twenty years. I wouldn't know him on the street if I passed him. I couldn't pick him out of a line-up of six men with dark, curly hair. He might not even have dark, curly hair anymore. He might not . . .

My dad's voice says, "Cut your losses. Don't invest again until you're absolutely certain."

My mom's face looks up at me, my mom's face under the layers of pancake and age, and out of her old purple wrinkled lips my mom's voice says, *"Sing for me, honey, wouldja? One song. You got such a sweet voice. Sing for your old mom."*

And I turn my face to the sunless sky and close my eyes and think of a faceless dark-haired boy and I sing . . .

TREVOR SCHMIDT is an actor, director, playwright, and designer. His previously published plays include *Just* (in *Hot Thespian Action!*) and *Tales from the Hospital* (in *Staging Alternative Albertas*). Recent plays include: *Folie a Deux* (for the Maggie Tree), *Super Power* (for ATCO), *Dragula* (with Darrin Hagen for Guys in Disguise), and the upcoming *Cleopatra's Sister* (for Northern Light Theatre). He was most recently seen in *Coffee Dad, Chicken Mom and the Fabulous Buddha Boi* in New York's Frigid Festival 2009, and received an Outstanding Performance trophy at the Elizabeth Sterling Haynes Awards for the same show at the Edmonton Fringe. He is the artistic director of Northern Light Theatre, has co-created and appears regularly with Guys in Disguise, and was a member of the Loud & Queer company at Workshop West for many years—in fact, he was likely in many of the plays in this anthology!

The River
MICHAELA WASHBURN

And it pierced her

but this time in her grief came a whole new self unfolded,
unfolded in the buckling over of and in the silent exhales of deep
    wailing,
unfolded in the overwhelming desperation to cling to familiar smells
and handwriting and bingo dabbers.
Anything that might hold a memory,
that might bring back her Mother if even for a brief moment.

It mostly came in the middle of the night this kind of grief,
and for weeks everything seemed to happen in the middle of the night,
as sleep seemed haunted
and now she knew a loneliness like she'd never known before.

At times she would strain to hear her Dad, in the room across
the hall, crying himself to sleep. She wasn't sure and so rather
than pretend to be going to the washroom so she could see for
herself, she would lie there and listen to the dark.

Morning would come and Grandfather Sun would shine and she
would greet him with her gratitude and take a deep breath.
Yet now the world somehow looked different.

Everything still in its same place, the grass still green, the clouds still billowy and white.
Except now there was a huge hole in the sky.
She couldn't see it, but she could feel it, the weight of it.

She carries her grief and her memories and her words like a warrior, only now she is not as sure what it is she is fighting for.
Is it peace? Is it children? Is it love?
For although they are all one in the same to her,
her map is now inside out as she wanders,
trying to understand the loss of her Mother
and thus of her connection to Mother Earth.

She watches through the window at the beautiful day.
Maybe she even walks briefly to do an errand or two.
But then, once again, she retreats
and looks through her phone book over and over only to call no one.

She sits with her words and attempts to make sense.
She lives with a great storyteller from whom she is constantly inspired.
So she speaks now and then and sends her words around too.

Confused by the times she gets no response, she sometimes tricks herself into thinking it is because she must walk alone.
Alone through the fire and then through the rain.

So she walks.

Earlier today it was as though a voice said, "Stop what you are doing and let me hold you a second" . . . so she did. She put down her toothbrush and hugged herself.

And with one hand on her own cheek she cried . . . and then
stopped that too. It felt as though it was her mama's hand, but
then she wondered if she was only wanting it to be.
Still she allowed the moment to continue for another moment more.
Then she picked up her toothbrush, looked in the mirror, and
wiped her face dry.

"They will come," she thought to herself,
"these moments and these tears will come and they will be more of
what fills the river that is now a constant current in your life."
This river that began long before she knew of it,
the river of grief that would carry the lanterns of her Kokum and
her Sister and now her Mother.
And many dear dear friends too.

And she talks to herself,
not to want to jump,
but to trust that her time will come when it is meant to come,
when she too will become part of the river that is the current in
another's soul.

So for now,
with all that she has learned and walked through,
she simply prays
for the river to be calm.

A Métis artist from the small town of Leduc, Alberta, MICHAELA WASHBURN
is proud to be of English, Irish, French, and Cree descent. She is a
graduate, on scholarship, from Toronto's Second City's Conservatory
Program and is now based in Toronto. Over the years, her many tal-
ents have included writing, counselling, workshop facilitation, theatre,

film, television, stand-up comedy, hosting, clown, and improvisation. Michaela has been nominated for the 2011 K.M Hunter Artist Award for Theatre and a Dora Mavor Moore Award for Outstanding Performance by a Female in a Principal Role for her work in the premiere of Judith Thompson's *Such Creatures* (Theatre Passe Muraille). Michaela is grateful for her family and friends, for the seven generations before her and the seven who are to come, for helping her to find her voice and her place in this circle.

continental divide
BEAU COLEMAN

a video installation

in 16 sequences

(an excerpt)

SEQUENCE 1

WALL I	WALL II
	Not only because—
I understood too late.	
	I was too much confused.
	I hope that these days don't become sand in a desert, but fertile earth.
Ah! Send me.	
	Your presence was like a good friend for me.

WALL III   WALL IV

Because now.

     I lack words
     with which
     to express.

I felt myself
like a stranger

     I wait—

     I don't want to forget.

of an angel!

SEQUENCE 2

WALL I

Writing is the body,
the hands
the voice
the reality
the connection
I'm looking for reality
the concrete reality
the body

of two thoughts,
feelings,
glances
of two lifetimes.

WALL II

Thousands of miles!

To live (to love)
perhaps
is a magic ritual
that sometimes
runs
and sometimes not . . .

What is it that is
not being expressed?

Do you want a word?

WALL III   WALL IV

                  Lack of time.

Where to begin?

                  At the first moment
I don't know why   you caught my eyes—
but it was as though
you were in a circle of light
in a circle of silence–

so I sat near you
and I started feeling
as though–

nothing
in another space and time.

                  of two thoughts,
                  feelings,
                  glances
                  of two lifetimes.

WALL I	WALL II

It is our soul,
our enthusiastic
and universal soul—

There was not
the season.

              Maybe something
              more precious is coming—
              maybe not . . .

Who are you?

              I would like to say
              what I feel,
              but that is very
              irrational . . .

It is strange to have the
feeling to know somebody
but to have to remember
you don't know this person.

My thoughts, my feelings . . .
it is all a very intricate question.

WALL III

WALL IV

I'm amazed and
frightened.

There was not the
time—

and when it is not the
proper season
all is impossible.

I can't miss you.

Who am I?

You are in my mind
like a possibility of
beauty, attention,
strength, tranquility . . .
a particular combination
of feelings, a world that
for me now has
your name.

You meet
whom you
need to
meet.
I'll do
everything
to go on with
knowing.

WALL I   WALL II

                          Why don't you
                          ask me
                          your thousands
                          of questions?

It happened
something which
hurt me————

I only want
that you know that.

                          NUMBER THREE

3 years ago I began . . .

I learned much
through love.

                          Now,
                          no more words . . .

WALL III   WALL IV

                             I felt and I'm feeling
                             many, many
                             moments
                             of regret.

3 years I started . . .   3 years ago I met . . .

                             I've been destroyed
                             but then rebuilt.

I'll answer all your questions.

I would like to be able
to tell you my
dreams.

SEQUENCE 3

WALL I	WALL II
	I did not know I could suffer so much for love.
	Even just a thought, a feeling, a fragment of something . . .
	The confusion became clearness and quiet then, strength, then, enthusiasm.
	It is now a language of feeling . . .

SEQUENCE 4

WALL I	WALL II
(chant)	(chant)
(chant)	(chant)

WALL III	WALL IV
The third year has been about absence.	
It was quite bitter!	
I could not love I wanted only solitude. I needed to be alone . . .	
I wanted to rebuild in me, where there was a waste land . . .	
If I have the strength to change a wound into riches it is because a person whom I did not know has been near my soul.	

WALL III	WALL IV
	(chant)
All is magic.	(chant)

BEAU COLEMAN is a performance/installation artist and theatre director whose work has been performed and exhibited across North America, Europe, and in parts of Africa, Australia, and Asia. She has made works for a diverse range of locations and contexts, whether they be situated in galleries, theatres, suspended over rivers, or projected onto buildings. Previous creations have included live art, spoken word, digital media, site-specific performance, video, dance, and new media installation. Themes of isolation, suspension, identity, memory, intimacy, and sexuality are interrogated in her work. Beau received her training at the National Theatre School of Canada and is a graduate of the Yale School of Drama. She is on faculty at the University of Alberta, where she conspires to blur the boundaries between the various art disciplines.

continental divide: a video installation in 16 sequences was originally commissioned by Loud & Queer and was subsequently exhibited in 1995 as part of FAVA's Instant Intimacy. It later received solo and group exhibitions at the Galleria di Arte Contemporanea, Trento, Italy, in 1998 and as part of INMPR/Institute of New Media Performance Research's Binary Bodyplay at the Lewis Eton Gallery in Guildford, United Kingdom, in 1999, which went on to tour the United Kingdom and Morocco.

Maybe
CHANDRA MAYOR

Your bathroom window faces east, and sitting on the edge of the tub you can't see the sun sink broken to the ground. But you can see darkness blurring the edges of the buildings around you, the graffiti fading into brick, its cryptic message lost for the night. Strangers in black coats stained with snow are only visible in the flash of a white neck, the gash of a red scarf. Somewhere there are women standing in a circle, ankle deep in snow, holding candles and maybe singing, maybe standing silently, clouds of breath rising into the night.

You don't know this. You have locked the door. The water is running, angry against the chipped enamel, and you have finished crying for the night. Something is in your hand, maybe a washcloth soaked in icy water pressed deep into the swollen flesh of your cheek, maybe a sharp silver rectangle, its crimson smudge wiped clean against your thigh. Punishment and redemption eventually begin to look the same, the sharp wet tang like red wine against your tongue, the brief limp and the scar from your own complicit hand.

There is a cup of amber liquid on the edge of the tub beside you, whiskey or tea or both. There are brown towels onto which you've sewn blue stars, your fingers holding the silver needle that rises up and sinks down through the fabric, thick as skin. Your locked doors keep nothing out and nothing in. On the other side there is raging or silence, the fist pounding on wood that insists you come out, or maybe the banging and longing to be let in. Either way you are locked up tight, your breath compressed in the top of your chest, your mind dancing and jerking like a dying fish.

Tomorrow night there will be no women in the snow, and you will still be curled up in a corner of the dirty bathroom. Maybe you will have memorized a phone number and maybe it is the black phone you hold in your hand. You will hang up when someone answers, the sound of a woman's voice too much like your own, your own voice with no words for what has been done, for what you do, for what the difference is. You will hear a busy tone and not bother calling back.

You let your fingertips trail in rage, in the water in the tub, in the vulnerable velvet behind your knees. You think of fragile things, snowglobes and porcelain figures. You think of fast things, snowmobiles and stolen cars. You think of people who steal, of talk-show hosts who steal the word *shame* and push you further back into wordlessness. You think of half-remembered men who steal the word *wonder* and leave you with blank spots in your head and mysterious scars on your flesh. You think of police who steal the word *safety* and make flinty jokes about you as they walk away. You think of everyone who steals the word *victim* and leaves you on the other side of something vast and impenetrable, voiceless. You open your mouth and scream and maybe your kids come running and maybe your boyfriend backs away and maybe something shatters in the air and the empty house says nothing.

You pick up the razor. You pick up the needle. You pick up the broken finger and dial again. Someone answers. You open your mouth. You wait to hear what you will say.

CHANDRA MAYOR is a Winnipeg writer and editor. Her short-story collection *All the Pretty Girls* received a Lambda Literary Foundation Award for Best Lesbian Fiction. She is also the author of the Carol Shields Winnipeg Book Award-winning novel *Cherry*. A former poetry editor for *Prairie Fire* and *CV2*, her writing frequently appears in journals and anthologies, including *Post-Prairie: New Prairie Writing* (eds. Robert Kroetsch and Jon Paul Fiorentino) and *Persistence: All Ways Butch and Femme* (eds. Ivan Coyote and Zena Sharman).

Skinflute Sonata

GERALD OSBORN

*Lights flash. Music pounds. The scent of sweat and Obsession wafts
through the air. It's a gay nightclub. And its denizens are writhing
on the dance floor. Jerome sits in a dark corner nursing an imported
beer. He's late thirties/early forties, marginally attractive in a run-of-
the-mill sort of way. Seated beside him is another figure, arms folded,
face buried in his arms. But more on him later. Jerome observes the
proceedings, tries to go with the flow. He catches someone's eye, offers
the friendliest of smiles, and is rebuffed immediately. He sits back
in his chair, sighs.*

Jerome: I must be out of my mind. Otherwise why would I keep
putting myself through this? The hideous music . . . the
stench of stale beer . . . and them . . . *(indicates the
dancing denizens.)* Their buffed bods. Their beautiful faces. Their fuck-you attitudes. Just look at 'em
a-hoppin' and a-boppin' across the dance floor. Never
looking in my direction. Never even acknowledging my
presence. Never once letting me join in their reindeer
games.

The question is, Why do I bother? Feels like I'm running my ego over a cheese grater here. And for what?
These guys. Every year their faces get younger, their asses
get shapelier. Meanwhile I'm developing this wonderful
lived-in look.

Rusty: Will you stop already? You're gonna make me weep! *(The figure at the table lifts his head to reveal the face of Rusty, the personification of Jerome's male member.)*

So . . . how's it hangin'? Oops! Guess I'd be the obvious one to answer that. *(Rusty flops his head onto his left shoulder.)* A little to the left, I'd say.

Jerome: Look, I'm not in the mood right now.

Rusty: But that's my job, buddy-boy. To get you in the mood *(indicating the dance floor.)* Just take a look at all this talent. There's so many loaded baskets here you'd think we were at the Easter Parade. Easter Parade . . . baskets . . . d'you get it?

Jerome is unmoved.

Okay, I'm a cock, not a comedian. So sue me.

Jerome: This is ridiculous. I should be home doing laundry. Or reading a good book. *(He takes a swig of beer.)*

Rusty: Hey, go easy on the Heineken, wouldja? You don't buy beer, you rent it. An' believe me I know whereof I speak.

Jerome: Instead I'm being lectured to by my junk. *(He takes another swig.)* Gonna finish this, then we're outta here. If we hurry we can catch the tail end of *Letterman*.

Rusty: What's the rush? The night is young.

Jerome: So's everybody in this room. With one notable exception.

Rusty: Okay, maybe these days you are sporting a few extra sags 'n' wrinkles. Big deal. They're hardly noticeable—

Jerome: Especially when moving rapidly toward the exit. *(He rises, ready to go.)*

Rusty: Forget it. I'm not leavin'.

Jerome: You don't understand. I can't cope with this right now—

Rusty: No, you don't understand. I'm pumped . . . I'm primed . . . I'm rarin' to go!

Jerome: Truth be told I haven't been intimate with anyone in a long time—

Rusty: Duh! Why d'you think I've got this pained expression on my face? But don't worry. With me ridin' shotgun it'll all come back to you like that! *(Snaps fingers.)* Cast your eyes on that dance floor. What is it you see?

Jerome: Rejection . . . humiliation . . . despair—

Rusty: Not gonna make this easy, are ya?

Jerome: These guys won't give me the time of day. That's why I'm declaring a moratorium on sex. I mean, who needs this shit anyway?

Rusty: I do! I do!

Jerome: Well, I'm doing fine without. Got my job, my condo, my DVD collection.

Rusty: Big whoop!

Jerome: And while it's not exactly exciting, it's familiar and comfortable and safe. 'Til you rear your ugly head—

Rusty: Hey!

Jerome: And suddenly you're dragging me off to this tawdry sleazepit.

Rusty: Draggin'? I may have pointed the way, but you're here 'cause you wanna be! *(Rusty abandons the table.)*

Jerome: What are you doing?

Rusty: *(Moving out into the audience.)* There's wall-to-wall manflesh out here. Bound to be something to get your nipples in a twist. *(Rusty spies a particular audience member, points him out to Jerome.)* Huh? Huh?

Jerome: Nice smile, but I pass.

Rusty: *(Zeroing in on another one.)* How 'bout him?

Jerome: Sweet, but no.

Rusty: Him? Him? *Her?* Work with me, buddy-boy. None of these guys got cooties—'cept maybe him.

Jerome: You're wasting my time. This is hopeless.

Rusty: Just pretend we're in the meat aisle at Sobeys. Always does the trick for me. *(Rusty moves through the crowd likening various audience members to meat products.)* Over here you got your corned beef . . . your beef jerky . . . your premium bologna—

Jerome: What a healthy approach to sex. No wonder I'm so well adjusted.

Rusty: *(Rusty's ardour is rising.)* Get a load of the pastrami . . . the summer sausage . . . the bun-length all-beef wieners— *(He is caught up in the excitement.)* Leg of lamb . . . outside round steak . . . inside round steak . . . sirloin tip—*(Rusty catches his breath, then:)* Is it hot in here or is it just me?

Jerome: It's just you.

Rusty: What's your problem anyway? Was a time we were like this *(crosses his fingers,)* fellow explorers in a deep dark jungle of filth and frolic. Now I hardly recognize you. Dontcha remember all those sweaty one-night stands?

Jerome: I remember plunging into a lot of overwhelming situations—

Rusty: Wasn't it swell? All the intensity . . . the electricity . . . the incandescence—*(A triumphant howl.)*

Jerome: And I'll admit there were some great times. I also recall the frustration . . . the heartbreak . . . the embarrassment—

Rusty: Say what?

Jerome: Of being treated like something from the meat aisle at Sobeys. Kept waiting for some great romance to develop—

Rusty: Hey, man, I gave it my best shot, okay?

Jerome: Of course I blamed myself. Thought I was no good . . . that I was lacking in some major way.

Rusty: Now that's just silly.

Jerome: Like maybe I wasn't smart enough—

Rusty: What a buncha bunkum!

Jerome: Or maybe I wasn't good-looking enough—

Rusty: What a load of bumfluff!

Jerome: Or maybe I was a little lacking . . . below the belt.

Rusty: Come again?

Jerome: Well, I always felt that things might've worked out better if I'd had a tad more to offer down there—no offence.

Rusty: None taken. I appreciate your honesty. And I respect you for sharin'. One thing, though.

Jerome: What's that?

Rusty: You're insane! *(Rusty drops to the floor and does several one-armed push ups.)* I am a juggernaut, a leviathan, a behemoth!

Jerome: Take it easy! You're gonna pop a blood vessel! *(Jerome tries to help Rusty to his feet. Rusty rejects Jerome's assistance.)*

Rusty: If I'm such an embarrassment to you—

Jerome: You're not—

Rusty: Then maybe you oughta just deal with the problem once and for all!

Jerome: How—

Rusty: There's a host of amazing penile enlargement techniques available.

Jerome: Such as?

Rusty: Cock pumps. You know, those tubes with the vacuum dealies that—

Rusty puffs out his cheeks until his head almost explodes. Then he lets the air out quite audibly in the general direction of Jerome's face.

Or those weights they attach that pull you and yank you and stretch you—*(Rusty stands on tiptoes, stretching out as tall as he possibly can.)*

Jerome: I pass.

Rusty: Of course there's always surgery. Where they make this slit right down the middle—

Jerome: Ouch!

Rusty: And install an inflatable device! *(Makes a huge expansive gesture with accompanying inflating sound effect.)* Means you can screw and make balloon animals at the same time!

Jerome: Forget I said anything. *(Jerome becomes distracted by an offstage presence.)* Besides, it's all academic now. Time's little tweaks and nudges took care of my prime rib status long ago. I've accepted it. You oughta do the same.

Rusty: Okay. I know when I'm licked. What say we duck out of here?

Jerome: Now you're talking. *(Jerome steals a glance at the offstage presence.)*

Rusty: Maybe we can stop by the Triple X Emporium, check out the peep show.

Jerome: Uh . . . no.

Rusty: But they're open 24/7.

Jerome: I just don't think—

Rusty: You never wanna take me anywhere!

Jerome: It's really not my style.

Rusty: And what, pray tell, is your style? It's been so long I bet you don't even remember! *(Jerome takes another look at the offstage presence.)* Hey, I'm talkin' here!

Jerome: Wish he'd stop staring.

Rusty: Who?

Jerome: The guy with all the tattoos.

Rusty: Which Guy-With-All-the-Tattoos? There's only eight million of 'em.

Jerome: Sitting by the pool table.

Rusty: *(Matter-of-factly.)* You mean the one comin' on to you?

Jerome: Huh? What? You're off your nut!

Rusty: I know that look, Budski—

Jerome: But why would he—

Rusty: There's a glint in his eye—

Jerome: I mean how could he—I mean—it's me!

Rusty: He's just itchin' to take a ride on the Baloney Pony Express—

Jerome: No. I just remind him of someone, that's all.

Rusty: Leaving now for all points south of the border! AH-WOO-GAH!

Jerome: Stop that!

Rusty: Hey, I'm only trying to save you from a life of excessive masturbation.

Jerome: But what's the point? Even if we did hook up, it'd just turn out like all the others—plenty of shattered glass, twisted metal fragments, and a chalk outline on the highway. I can't take that risk. *(He steals one last look at the Guy.)* Gotta admit he's pretty cute, though. Not too young. Not too old. Are those dimples I see?

Rusty: Affirmative.

Jerome: And he looks intelligent—like he's read a book or two.

Rusty: If one of 'em's *The Joy of Gay Sex* then you're laughin'.

A brief pause as Jerome comes to a shocking realization.

Jerome: Oh gawd, I think I'm in love.

Rusty: Let's not get carried away.

Jerome: I know it sounds crazy—

Rusty: Uhh yeah!

Jerome: But suddenly I can picture the two of us together in our twilight years on some beachfront property holding hands, sipping wine, gazing contentedly into the shimmering sunset—

Rusty: Maybe you oughta fuck him first and make the Freedom 55 plans a little further down the road.

Jerome: *(Another coy glance in the Guy's direction.)* Eye contact! *(He turns away abruptly.)* Holy shit! You're right. There's a definite glint. What should I—

Rusty: *(Mouthing the words.)* Go for it!

Jerome shoots the Guy a come-hither look, then flirts shamelessly. It is obvious the reaction is favourable.

Jerome: This is astounding! This is phenomenal! Looks like we'll be seeing some action tout de suite!

Rusty: Wow! Despite all your squawkin' this means a helluva lot to you, doesn't it?

Jerome: You betcha. And I refuse to screw it up this time! Gonna be ruthless! Gonna show no mercy! That's why I'm counting on you!

Rusty: Say no more. I got some new moves that're so hot they'll make the ink in his tattoos run!

Jerome: WA-HOO!

Rusty: YEE-HAH! So what're we waitin' for? *(Rusty launches into a little shadow boxing.)* Lemme at him! Just let me at him! I . . . Ohhhh!

Rusty loses his footing.

Jerome: What is it?

Rusty: Dunno. Suddenly I'm feeling kinda woozy. Can barely keep my head up.

Jerome: Not a good sign. *(Distracted by the Guy.)* Ahhh, would you look at that smile? *(Jerome gives a little wave. Jerome staggers.)*

Rusty: Hate to be a party pooper, but the room is spinning! *(Rusty collapses. Jerome catches him and eases him onto the floor.)*

Jerome: Geez! What d'you suppose is wrong?

Rusty: Beats me. Maybe I forgot to eat.

Jerome: *(Attention returning to the Guy.)* He's getting up! I think he's . . . yes . . . he's coming over! *(To Rusty.)* You gonna be okay? Tell me you're gonna be okay!

A coughing jag. Rusty is Camille on her deathbed.

Rusty: The prognosis is not good. We're talkin' wizened nub here. May be in danger of shrinking away altogether.

Jerome: Now he's pushing through the crowd. He'll be here in a matter of seconds. Is there anything I can—*(Rusty reaches up, pulls Jerome in very close.)*

Rusty: *(In a raspy whisper.)* You know I could get well again . . .

Jerome: Oh yeah?

Rusty: . . . if somebody just believed in me.

Jerome: And that's all it'd take?

Rusty: Uh huh.

Jerome: So how do I—

Rusty: Maybe you could . . . clap your hands—

Jerome: *(Realizing it's all a scam.)* Oh brother!

Rusty: *(Weakly.)* Hey, if you're not interested—*(Rusty passes out with a moan.)*

Jerome: Okay . . . okay . . . *(Jerome plays along and claps with his hands in a half-assed manner.)*

Jerome: I believe in you. There. Now can we get this show on the road?

Rusty: Not good enough! *(Rusty has another coughing jag, horks up a lugie. It isn't pretty.)* Looks like I'm down for the count! Headin' for that big jockstrap in the sky!

Jerome: I dunno what else I can do—

Rusty: What about—? *(Indicates the audience.)*

Jerome: Oh no. I could never—*(Rusty has another coughing jag. With no other options, Jerome turns to the audience.)*

Ordinarily I wouldn't bother you with something so trivial, but my sex life's going down the toilet so if you could please humour "Dinkerbell" here and—*(Jerome leads the audience in a round of applause.)*

Rusty: Oh . . . oh my . . . I'm not sure but . . . I think . . . yes, yes . . . blood's pumpin' . . . tissue's swellin'—*(Like Popeye after downing a can of spinach, Rusty rebounds to his former glory.)* I'm cured! I'm cured!

Jerome: Just in the nick of time. *(Jerome and Rusty glance outward expectantly, but the Guy has disappeared.)*

Rusty: Hey, where'd he go?

Jerome: Dunno. Something better must've come along.

Rusty: Oh shit.

Jerome: Guess I should've seen it coming.

Rusty: You blame me, dontcha?

Jerome: No.

Rusty: 'Cause I was just kiddin' around, payin' you back for that "wee willy winky" crack—

Jerome: It's okay—

Rusty: But I never meant to louse you up in perpetuity!

Jerome: I'm used to it, really.

Rusty: Ought to just lop me off right here and now! It'd serve me right!

Jerome: Probably all for the best anyway. About the size thing—

Rusty: Yeah?

Jerome: It's nothing personal. Guys always want it bigger. Bigger car. Bigger condo. Bigger paycheque. You could be a yardstick, I still wouldn't be satisfied. So if I hurt you in any way—

Rusty: I'm a big boy. I can handle it. Look, how's about we head home, spend a little "together" time?

Jerome: Whatcha got in mind?

Rusty: Well, you can pop in one of your porn DVDs—

Jerome: Okay.

Rusty: Then you can slip between the sheets—

Jerome: Mm hmm.

Rusty: I can slip out of your gonch—

Jerome: Uh huh.

Rusty: And you can pummel the porksword 'til the wee hours of the morning. Not my idea of a fun date, but you've had a rough day so I'm relaxing my standards.

Jerome: That's a very generous offer—

Rusty: I know.

Jerome: But for now, I'm staying put.

Rusty: Why? Oh, buddy-boy, if you think Guy-With-All-the-Tattoos is comin' back, 'fraid you're cruisin' for a bruisin'.

Jerome: No, he's long gone. But at least he gave me a second look. Which means maybe I'm not the chewed-up piece of gristle I thought I was.

Rusty: You do have your charms.

Jerome: So why not stick around awhile? Ya never know what might develop.

Rusty: You're the boss.

Jerome: Yeah, right.

Rusty: Ya know, from here on in, I'm makin' a resolution: to keep a lower profile.

Jerome: Why's that?

Rusty: I dunno, to take the pressure off, give you some breathing room.

Jerome: That might be helpful.

Rusty: But I'm not abandoning you—

Jerome: Of course not.

Rusty: If you have any concerns whatsoever, you know where to find me.

Jerome: Now that you mention it, been noticing this little premature ejaculation problem—Kidding! Just kidding!

Rusty: I may be a teensy-weensy dick, but you're a great big asshole!

Jerome: C'mere, you little zippersnake. *(Jerome pulls Rusty into a bear hug, looks out on the dance floor.)* Look at 'em all a-hoppin' and a-boppin' 'cross the dance floor. Aren't they . . . fabulous?

Lights fade.

Grizzled old theatre veteran GERALD OSBORN has premiered numerous plays at the Edmonton Fringe Festival, including *Scream Play*, *baby-HEAD*, *Toying With Dinky*, and the notorious *ALBERT EAT POO*. His work has been presented by Jagged Edge, Catalyst, Northern Light, Workshop West, CBC Radio, and in such exotic locales as Vancouver, Calgary, Medicine Hat, and Whitecourt.

For the past two decades he has been employed by Fringe Theatre Adventures. At the 2006 Sterling Awards, he received the Margaret Mooney Award for Outstanding Achievement in Administration. When fate hooked Gerald up with Loud & Queer, he discovered the perfect outlet for the saucier side of his writing. Creating plays about peep shows, phone sex, and talking penises also allowed him to write about love, loneliness, and what it is to be human. The Loud & Queer experience has given him the opportunity to work with some of the leading lights of the Edmonton theatre scene and has provided him with the inspiration for such Sterling-nominated Fringe hits as *Adam Butterfly* and *Meat Farce*. Gerald would like to thank Darrin Hagen and Ruth Smillie, who were there at the beginning.

This is a picture of me

T.L. COWAN

This is a picture of me, 8 years old.
This is the dress of yellow wool.
These are the tights that failed.
This is me ripping out the sagging crotch with my teeth.

This is a picture of me, 12 years old.
This is what happens when you are 5 feet, 11 inches tall in Grade 7.
The other students are standing on benches.
You can see me, right over here, standing on the floor.
On the other side of the picture is the teacher, also standing on
    the floor.
All 5 feet, 4 inches of her.

This is a picture me, 16 years old.
Look, here around my neck you can see the
necklace I received as a gift from my boyfriend.
It had a real diamond in it.
It was small but real.
He was such a nice guy.
Such a normal guy.
Such a normal necklace.

This is a picture of me, standing in my figure skates dressed as a
    Hoola Girl.

This is a picture of me, standing in my figure skates dressed as a Christmas Tree.

This is a picture of me, standing in my figure skates dressed as a Teddy Bear.

This is a picture of me, standing with my figure-skating trophy.

This is a picture of me, 11 years old.

This is the sweatshirt, blue, almost new, that came from the girl down the block.

This is the polo shirt, white with green and blue stripes, pink collar, from her brother.

These are the pants, white cotton, that were left in a box at our front door one day.

These are the earrings bought for 99 cents at the corner store. I put them in too soon after

I got my ears pierced and my ears got infected and bled.

This is a picture of my baptism.

This is a picture of my first communion.

In both pictures I am wearing white dresses that my mother made from her wedding dress.

This is a picture of me, 3 years old.

I am barefoot, wearing a green and yellow dress and carrying my first purse.

This is a picture of me, singing in a choir.

Like everyone else, I am wearing a white blouse, a blue scarf, and a denim skirt.

Unlike everyone else, I am wearing a white slip, which is sticking out from under my denim skirt.

I am also wearing beige control-top pantyhose. I am 9.

Here is my first picture as a lesbian.
I am wearing a goddess necklace, many women-
symbol earrings, a non-supportive sports
bra, a baggy T-shirt tucked into baggy jeans and a studded
belt. My head is shaved and I am wearing no makeup.
Next to my two sisters I look pretty butch.

This is picture of all of us by the waterfalls.
The leaves have turned colour and we are all wearing wool sweaters.

This is a picture of me, topless, at the Michigan Womyn's festival.
I am wearing a colourful hat because I thought it would make me
    stand
out and my glasses that I thought made me look smart, both of
which I thought would increase my chances of getting laid. I was
    wrong.

This is a picture of my first lesbian truck.
The dykey one in the driver's seat is my girlfriend.
The truck kept us together for quite
some time after we'd stopped having sex.

This is the prom dress.
These are the shoes.
This is the ribbon.
This is the shotglass.

This is the dress I wore to my first wedding as a lesbian.
I also wore very large, practical shoes as a radical
political statement against femininity.
This is my mother's voice, strained and sad.

There was a lot of hair in the nineties.
This is the fake tan from a bottle.
This is the upside-down blow-drying.
This is the hairspray.
These are the shoes carried home, walking barefoot
many blocks in Ottawa on New
Year's Eve, feet frozen but no longer cramped.

These are the hiking boots.
This is the fleece jacket.
This is the tent.
This is the headlamp.
And here is the stovetop espresso-maker.

These are my varicose veins.
These are my broken toenails.
This is a picture of what my ass used to look like.
This is my mother's ring.
This is my sister's razor.
These are your Venetian blinds, sun shining stripes on my naked body.

This is my cigarette.
This is my single-malt scotch, neat.
This is the trace of your sadness.
Here is your common sense.

This is a picture of me, 16 years old.
If you look closely you can see that I am no longer a virgin.
This is the un-lubricated condom.

This is a picture of you and your best friend.
I'm sorry I slept with him. It was so easy.

This is the band I liked when I lived in Halifax.
This is that German woman, whose name I forget.
Yes, like me, she is tall and beautiful.
This is a picture of me and the German woman making
out on the counter in the lady's bathroom so that we could
look at ourselves in the mirror. We are totally hot.

This is my credit card balance.
This is the day I stopped wearing earrings.
This is what I would look like if I could go all the way and be a
    punk.
This is what I look like instead, kind of boring.

This is the game we played.
If you remember correctly, you will recall that I won.
This is the fight for equality with the television set:
Saturday Night at the Movies vs. *Hockey Night in Canada*.

These are the meals we ate.
These are the dishes I broke by accident.
Here are the ones I broke on purpose.
This is the long table where we ate, but never fucked
because we agreed it wasn't sturdy. This is the counter.
Chopping block. Knives. Cookbooks. Dried beans.
This is our lesbian life.

This is my pocketknife.
The large blade sticks, but the small one is sharp
and cuts well.

This is the look on your face.
This is a close-up of the blackheads on my nose and forehead.

This picture is empty because we were moving when it was taken.
This is my scorn. Here is my anger.
My lust is in the corner over there behind the bookshelf.

This is a picture of my next-door neighbour when I was 8.
This is her father's face trying to get us to unlock the bathroom
    door.
This is us in the bathroom, giving each other bubble baths.

This is the *Dirty Dancing* soundtrack. Cliché but very formative.
This is Demi Moore. This is Winona Ryder.
This is Rob Lowe. This is Allie Sheedy.
This is a picture of Mary Stewart Masterson.
This is Elizabeth Shue.

These are the men locked out of the house that
Thanksgiving when we got drunk and thought that
the feminist thing to do would be to teach them
a lesson for not offering to
do the dishes, especially after I had
made pumpkin pies from scratch.

This is a picture of me soon after,
deciding I would never bake for a man again.
These are the vegan brownies I made for our road trip.
This is the black bean hummus with spelt pita.

These are the single beds the Polish woman
wanted us to sleep in at her bed and breakfast.
These are the mattresses pushed together on the floor.
This is a picture of the Polish woman's face,
standing in the hallway, listening to the

sounds of you fucking me with a full fist.

This is how we left the sheets in the morning.

This is a picture of me, 10 years old.

I am in my pyjamas, sitting on my father's lap, reading a story.

He is asleep.

T.L. COWAN is a Queer feminist writer, performer, activist, and professor currently living in and between Saskatoon, Toronto, and Montreal. As an artist, she got her start in the booming spoken-word scene of Vancouver in the late 1990s and since then has been making work that plays with and interrogates the complexities of contemporary Queer femininity in performances that draw from cabaret, costume-based and alter-ego performance, spoken word, agit-prop theatre, stand-up comedy, video and sound art, and installation and intervention. These performances reflect an ongoing quasi-pseudo-autobiographical meditation on female composites, class mobility, sexuality, and style. T.L.'s work has been featured on pages and stages across Canada and internationally, including *Notebook Magazine, Matrix Magazine, Bent on Writing: Contemporary Queer Tales*, Montreal's Edgy Women Festival, the Glastonbury Festival of Contemporary Art, and Toronto's Festival of Original Theatre. Between 2002 and 2009, T.L. lived in Edmonton and happily performed many times at Loud & Queer.

The Island
TREVOR ANDERSON

I'm an independent Canadian filmmaker in Northern Alberta.

And believe it or not, sometimes I get fan mail. Uh-huh.

The best was an email I got from the United States of America. It said, "You fucking faggots. You're a disgrace to society. You should all be put on an island so you can give each other AIDS."

And when I read that, I thought, "Hm. Why not?"

I mean, doesn't that sound lovely? Our own island! A homo utopia. Like our own little Israel. A homeland for the assmunching diaspora.

Now, this idea of the island isn't exactly new. No. I grew up with it.

It was part of the rhetorical landscape of my small-town, prairie childhood.

Every so often you'd hear someone say, "They should all be put on an island." You know, it was almost a common thing to hear, in bars, on job sites. "Put 'em all on an island and sink it."

Sometimes I'd argue back, but because I was still in the closet that usually meant just pointing out how hard it would be to, you know, sink an island.

But this new island! Where we're all supposed to give each other AIDS! That's a way better idea.

Unprotected humping all day long? Uh . . . yes, please!

It'd be like the seventies all over again. But better, because . . . it's on an island!

And we could make up all the rules. Like, when people do get infected, they're raised to a greater status in society.

Treated like celebrities instead of sickos. Given the coolest tree huts and the strongest ape-masseurs.

We could ensure universal access to free, life-prolonging, anti-retroviral drug cocktails, served in coconuts with little umbrellas and huge wedges of pineapple!

And rum!

Rum!

And even if, with the best, most attentive medical care at our society's disposal, someone does get terminally sick from an HIV-related illness, well then we'll all gather round him at twilight, man . . .

. . . and cover him with moonflower blossoms . . .

. . . decorate his skin with rub-on sailor tattoos . . .

. . . and sing him torch songs to the rhythm of the pounding surf.

And then, just as he's taking his last breath . . .

. . . we'll huck him into the mouth of the volcano . . .

. . . and worship him as a god.

Yeah. It's a nice idea, Faggot Island.

But even in my fantasies, I can't stay there very long. To me, there's something about the place that seems, I dunno. Kinda lonely.

TREVOR ANDERSON is a self-taught independent filmmaker. His work has screened at many international film festivals, including Sundance, Berlin, Toronto, SXSW, Outfest, and AFI Fest. At Hot Docs, Trevor won the inaugural Lindalee Tracey Award, presented to "an emerging Canadian filmmaker working with passion, humour, a strong sense of social justice and a personal point of view." Trevor is also a founding member of The Wet Secrets, whose song "Secret March" was named by Grant Lawrence of CBC Radio 3 as one of the "Best Songs of the Decade." For more information, please visit dirtcityfilms.com.

Written, Directed and Performed by Trevor Anderson
Produced by Julia Rosenberg and Tyler Levine, January Films
Co-Produced by Trevor Anderson
Director of Animation: Jeff LeDrew, Rat Creek Design
Director of Photography: Wes Doyle, C.S.C.
Steadicam Operator: Brett Manyluk
Editor: Justin Lachance
Sound: John Blerot, Wolf Willow Sound
Original Music: Dwayne Martineau and Scott Davidchuk

Produced with a grant awarded by CTV's Bravo!FACT
(Foundation to Assist Canadian Talent)
Made with the support of the FAVA 2-Bits Commission and the
National Film Board of Canada's Filmmaker Assistance Program
Copyright 2009 January Films
For more information, visit dirtcityfilms.com

Acknowledgments

I was once warned that once you started naming people, you had to name them all. So I would like to thank every artist, director, designer, artistic director, general manager, actor, volunteer, sponsor, and audience member who has ever been involved in the many Loud & Queer Cabarets over the last twenty years. It is because of their passion and loyalty that L&Q has lasted as long as it has, and they can all take pride in what the event has become over the years. Thanks to Workshop West for giving L&Q a home for so long. A special tip of the hat goes to long-time audience member and sponsor Ronald Rowswell, who kept many of the programs from over the years, which allowed me to scan through the decades with ease while choosing material for this collection.

But in particular, I would like to extend my gratitude to Ruth Smillie, Jacquie Richardson, Brenda O'Donnell, and Kevin Hendricks for launching this adventure, and to Ruth DyckFehderau, Heather Zwicker, and Pamela Anthony for their insight into this anthology.

Lastly, thanks go to my L&Q co-host, Kristy Harcourt. For years she and I have literally had the best seats in the house, watching generations of artists take the stage. Not only has she kept the show moving forward in spite of my tendency to be distracted, but it was her encouragement in 1995 at L&Q that kept me writing. That very generosity of spirit is what I remember every time I work with a writer. The difference a small gesture can make to an emerging career is incalculable.

DARRIN HAGEN is a freelance playwright, writer, composer, performer, director, and drag artiste. For two decades he has been at the helm of the annual Loud & Queer Cabaret. He is also the artistic director of the award-winning independent theatre company Guys in Disguise, Canada's leading creators of cross-dressing comedies, and mentor to many emerging Queer writers in Canada and the US. He is the author of *The Edmonton Queen: The Final Voyage* and *Tornado Magnet: A Salute to Trailer Court Women*, both published by Brindle & Glass Publishing. Hagen's plays include *BitchSlap!*; *The Neo-Nancies: Hitler's Kickline*; *Buddy*; *With Bells On*; *The Glory, The Fury*; *Inventing Rasputin*; *Tornado Magnet*; and *The Edmonton Queen*. He has received seven Sterling Awards for his work in Edmonton theatre. *Buddy* was nominated for a Sterling Award for Outstanding New Play; *With Bells On* was nominated for a Betty Mitchell Award for Best New Play; and *The Edmonton Queen* received a Sterling Award for Outstanding New Fringe Work. Hagen also received an AMPIA for Best Male Host for his work on the Life Channel Series *Who's On Top?*

In 2005, Hagen was named as one of the 100 Edmontonians of the Century to mark the city's centennial, his name following alphabetically right after Wayne Gretzky. To the best of his knowledge, he's the only drag queen on that list. For more information on Guys in Disguise, visit guysindisguise.com.